THE ROCKING CHAIR BOOK

Overleaf: Porch rockers, Ocean Grove, New Jersey

THE ROCKING CHAIR BOOK

Ellen and Bert Denker
Foreword by Kenneth L. Ames

A Main Street Press Book
Published by Mayflower Books, Inc., U.S.A., New York

Contents

Foreword

Although Americans have been writing about their furniture for over a century, it is remarkable how few really good books have been produced. Most authors either repeat a familiar patter or devote their energies to showing why the pieces of furniture they like are better than the ones they don't. *The Rocking Chair Book* by Ellen and Bert Denker is a bright, promising exception to all this. An admirable example of solid and imaginative scholarship, it provides an impressive collection of information and insights about the rocking chair, a familiar but little-studied aspect of American material culture. By looking at this commonplace object in new ways the Denkers have helped us see a little more of the richness and complexity that surround us. And by showing how the rocking chair was developed, used, and altered in response to people's diverse needs, wants, and values, they have helped us better appreciate the complex maze of human factors that lie behind the seemingly ordinary objects of our own lives.

The Rocking Chair Book brings together a wealth of verbal and pictorial material that should appeal to collectors, dealers, furniture and interior designers, museum and historic house personnel, historians, and anyone interested in American homes and furnishings. But the book also contains much for those fascinated by the ways people interact with the objects around them. *The Rocking Chair Book* is that rare and precious accomplishment, a book on furniture that short-changes neither objects nor the people associated with them, but tries to understand the relationship between them. The Denkers have written an artifact history that is also a social history, a human history. For that they deserve both gratitude and praise.

The variety of objects assembled in *The Rocking Chair Book* is wonderful. The Denkers have selected their images with care and arranged them with sensitivity. Scores of photographs of rocking chairs record the extraordinary diversity of the form and the inventiveness of the human mind. I am particularly fascinated by the attempts of nineteenth-century inventors to design alternative methods of rocking. Some of these were remarkably successful; their descendants are still in production today. Other readers may be attracted to different chapters in the history of the rocking chair, but most will probably be impressed by the variety within the category of rocking chairs; it is amazing how many different kinds have been made over the years.

Even more exciting to me, however, are the well-chosen images of rocking chairs in different contexts: in parlors, bedrooms, and dining rooms; in a Shaker meeting room; on the porches of summer cottages and resorts; or hanging from the ceiling of a furniture store around the turn of the century. Other images indicate that by the middle of the nineteenth century the rocking chair had become associated with a vision of old-fashioned America. In a number of the Denkers' illustrations it figures as an icon for certain prized traits and values in American society. These illustrations of objects in their native habitat, so to speak, often with people, are valuable documents for anyone interested in how Americans lived and what they thought, felt, and believed.

The Rocking Chair Book is an intelligent and stimulating work offered modestly and without pretense. Comprehensive in its scope and generous in its judgments, it is dedicated to demonstrating the richness of the commonplace. Above all, it is a humane book about objects that touched the lives of millions of people. I hope it will be widely read and consulted.

Kenneth L. Ames
The Henry Francis du Pont Winterthur Museum

THE ROCKING CHAIR BOOK

Oh, never mind, I reckon I'm good enough just as I am.

2. "Oh, never mind, I reckon I'm good enough just as I am." This is one of a series of photographs of Mark Twain taken by Albert Bigelow Paine at Upton House, a summer place in New Hampshire that Twain rented in 1906.

Introduction

From the beginning to the end of life, the rocking chair will keep you cradled in its comforting sway. It will rock you as an infant, as a child, as a mother, when you are ailing or tired, when you are aging or sad, when you are thoughtful or restless, and when you have nothing better to do than rock and be happy. It keeps the joints loose and the organs healthy, soothes backaches, arthritis, and rheumatic pains, calms the nerves, and quiets babies. Perhaps no machine invented by man or woman has done so much good and given so much comfort.

In some ways the rocking chair is like the weather: everyone knows it exists but no one seems to know much about it. There are rumors of its beginnings. Brief homage is paid to it now and then in treatises on furniture. Three books extolling its virtues have been written during the last fifty years. None of them, however, has really dissected the phenomenon of the rocking chair, peeled back the layers of paint and time to take a long, hard look.

As a commodity, the rocking chair touches all sides of the furniture business—research and development, manufacture, and marketing. So each phase of its evolution reflects the growth of the chair industry. As an artifact, the rocking chair touches mechanisms deep within us—patterns of memory, taste, and satisfaction. So each facet of its use mirrors aspects of our own society, our very selves.

The rocking chair is an American invention and an American institution. It grew out of the mixture that is America. Not the mixture of peoples, but the web of time and place and freedom of the middle classes to pursue happiness and comfort in a most inexpensive and pleasing form, and—once that comfort was found—to test it, improve it, and cherish it.

During long years of service, the rocking chair has been painted, stenciled, upholstered, spindled, caned, engineered, patented, and loved in any and every form. It has rocked in bedrooms, back rooms, dining rooms, kitchens, parlors, and, perhaps most of all, on porches. It is at home in the city or country. It can be true to itself, or it can turn and become a lounge, a bed, a cradle, an ingenious air conditioner, a highchair and baby carriage, a trunk, or even a set of library steps. Whether faithful to the awkward grace of the original conception or disguised as a distinguished member of the latest upholstered parlor suite, the rocking chair is, indeed, a chameleon in the furniture world.

The history of the rocking chair is more than a lesson in an artifact's evolution. It is a story filled with the excitement of discovery and success, with humor and sadness, with the tenderness of a mother's sweet caresses and the loneliness of an old man's long afternoons, with the joys of childhood and the pleasures of retirement, with warm summer evenings on the front porch and cold winter mornings around the old stove. This is the story of the rocking chair from beginning to end.

3. *The Hobby Horse*, painted by Robert Peckham in Massachusetts about 1840. The rocking horse was essential for every wealthy child's playroom in the eighteenth and nineteenth centuries. Like many children's toys and games, it was a means of imitating fathers and older brothers who spent a good part of their lives on horseback. The hobby horse, a stick with a replica of a horse's head attached to one end, was known to the ancient Greeks, and its use by young boys was so characteristic of this stage in life that, for example, a French depiction of the seven ages of man printed in 1482 shows a youngster with a hobby horse. The rocking hobby horse, however, seems to be an invention of the mid-seventeenth century as there are English and German examples from that period.

1.

The Quest for Ease and Comfort

The rocking chair has been a widely popular type of chair since the early nineteenth century. Today, millions of American families keep at least one somewhere in the home. But how often has anyone considered its beginnings, and how much is really known about its early use? Where and when was this comfortable and comforting chair invented?

Writers on the subject agree that the earliest rocking chairs were those created by the addition of two curved pieces of wood to the legs of preexisting chairs. In 1928, Esther Fraser and Walter Dyer suggested that Benjamin Franklin was the first person to do this. They based their belief on remarks made by the Rev. Mr. Manasseh Cutler in his journal entry of July 13, 1787, regarding a visit to Franklin's house in Philadelphia. Describing Franklin's "curiosities and inventions," Cutler was particularly impressed with the American statesman's "great armed chair with rockers and a large fan placed over it with which he fans himself, keeps flies off, etc., while he sits reading, with only a small motion of his foot...."[1]

There is no doubt that Benjamin Franklin had a rocking chair, but that he was its inventor is wishful thinking at best. The myth was nurtured during the period in the study of American material culture when writers were happy to attribute all good American furniture to a few identified craftsmen and to credit the development of new, improved, and typically-American forms to

the imaginations of certain colorful patriots of the late eighteenth century. Cutler's journal entry may indeed refer to an invention of Franklin's, but it most likely implies a convenience related to the famous Philadelphian's rocking chair rather than the invention of the form itself. By the use of a foot pedal, the ingenious Franklin was able to activate an overhead fan as he rocked. Hence the rocking chair provided both a comfortable seat and an appropriate motion for activating the fan mechanism. Although Franklin was not the inventor of the rocking chair, he was surely one of the first persons to investigate the air-circulating potential associated with rocking chairs.

Evidence gleaned from inventories and craftsmen's account books indicates that the practice of adding rockers to chairs began much earlier than 1787, the date suggested by Fraser and Dyer's literal reading of Cutler's journal. Two early inventory entries, in fact, confirm that the rocking chair was certainly in use by the 1740s and suggest that its origin was even earlier. When William Templin died in 1742 in Charlestown, Chester County, Pennsylvania, his estate included a rocking chair. Similarly, John Gunn of Westfield, Massachusetts, had a rocking chair amongst his belongings in 1748. If the invention of the rocking chair occurred at a single point in time and space, these two references, being only six years and many miles apart, do not furnish any clues as to where and when that great event happened. In both instances the form is referred to quite plainly as a rocking chair. There is no suggestion that either of them was a curiosity. Because Gunn's rocking chair is listed with his tools at the end of the inventory, it may have been relegated to a storage area, which would have been an ignominious and rather unlikely end for anything very far out of the ordinary.[2]

We know, therefore, that the rocking chair was in use in the American colonies by the 1740s and that, while it was not used as a seating form in every household (rocking chairs do not appear frequently in eighteenth-century inventories), it was nonetheless neither particularly uncommon nor unusual. But that is about *all* we can deduce. Unfortunately, the inventor of the rocking chair and its time and place of invention are still unknown.

The question of why the rocking chair was invented is perhaps more intriguing than the when and where of it. Resolution of this question leads back through history to two seemingly unrelated artifacts—the cradle and the easy chair. The cradle is important because it rocks; the easy chair, on the other hand, because of its role in the history of the pursuit of a comfortable seat.

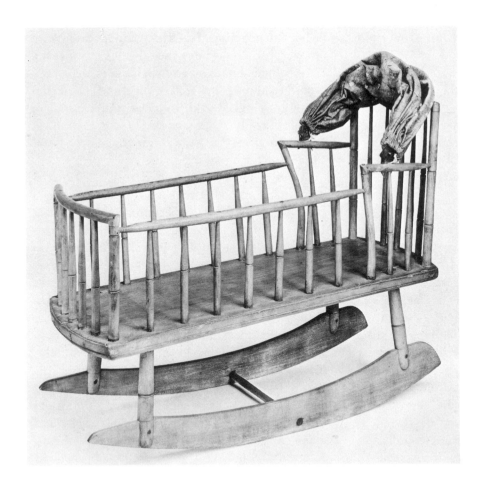

4. Rocking cradle probably made in Massachusetts, 1805-1825, and originally stained red. The end-to-end rocking of this unusual cradle seems on first thought to be a motion whereby "the child should be provoked to cast up his milk again." The orientation of the rockers is usually associated with rocking chairs rather than cradles. Spindles provided for better air circulation than that available with closed cradles. A number survive from Austria and Sweden.

14

Rocking Cradles

Prior to the development of the rocking chair, the only furniture form to possess rockers was the cradle. Although its invention is lost in antiquity, the use of the word "cradle" in the English language has been traced at least as far back as 1000 A.D. Illuminated manuscripts of the period show the cradle as being half a log hollowed out, which explains why none survive from this early date. By the fifteenth century it had attained a more familiar shape: a French illustration depicting the seven ages of man shows an infant in a cradle of four boards joined by corner posts and the whole raised on rockers similar to the example in figure 5. Fifteenth- and sixteenth-century "cradles of estate," used for the presentation of royal infants, are the oldest English cradles that remain. These include cradles that rock as well as those which swing freely within a frame.

Sixteenth-century physicians in England and France agreed that children placed in cradles benefitted in three ways: "The place for children to rest or sleep in best, is a cradle, because that thereof may grow a threefold commodity that is sleep sooner obtained, the parts through rocking better exercised, and the infant safer from such hurt preserved, as by having it in bed often happens." Rocking was considered useful for exercising the baby except "immediately after suckling," because "violent rocking [is] hurtful, lest that thereby the child should be provoked to cast up his milk again."[3]

Even into the eighteenth century the practice was to swaddle a newborn baby tightly in numerous linen cloths "to give his little Body a streight Figure, which is most decent and convenient for a man, and to accustom him to keep upon the Feet, for else he would go down upon all four, as most other Animals do." Swaddling also kept the infant warm as well as under control in the cradle where he was to have "his head a little

5. Cradle, probably made in a Moravian community in Pennsylvania, between 1730 and 1800. The small knobs on the sides were used as anchors to tie a swaddled baby into the cradle, as caretakers were admonished to do by Francois Mauriceau in the seventeenth century: "he must be bound and tied with strings, lest in rocking him, he fall out of his cradle." This particular cradle form, distinguished by square corner posts flaring out from bottom to top, long rockers attached through the ends of the corner posts, and scrolled head and foot panels with oblong hand holds, was popularly used by rural people in Austria and adjacent areas of Germany from the seventeenth through the early nineteenth centuries. A few American examples survive.

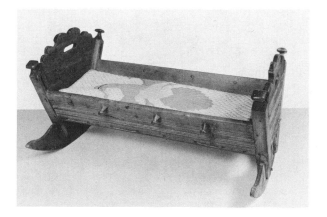

6. Hooded cradle made in the Delaware Valley, 1775-1820. Cold drafts were completely excluded from the infant by this type of hood. Protection against draughts was a continuing problem in homes until modern central heating was introduced in the mid-nineteenth century. In order to avoid the cold, caretakers were admonished to keep the infant tightly swaddled in linen cloths and near the fire. Many infants died from suffocation because they were kept too warm, which made the wicker cradle a more popular type than the cradle of dovetailed boards illustrated here. By the early nineteenth century stationary cribs came into more general use in reaction to violent cradle rocking "which puts the babe into a dazed condition, in order that he may not trouble those who have care of him."

raised up, that the excrements of his braine may the more easily flow and pass through the emunctoryes [i.e., nasal passages] thereof: And he must be bound and tied with strings, lest in rocking him he fall out of his cradle." The small knobs on the sides of seventeenth- and eighteenth-century cradles were used as anchors to tie the swaddled baby into the cradle.[4]

Rocking the infant in a cradle was recognized as an effective method of putting the baby to sleep. The practice, however, was often abused by wet nurses and caretakers, whom doctors denounced for their violent cradle rocking, "which puts the babe into a dazed condition, in order that he may not trouble those that have care of him." By the eighteenth century, experts began to speak out against the age-old cradle because the "ill-tempered nurse, who, instead of soothing the accidental uneasiness or indisposition to sleep of her baby, when laid down to rest, is often worked up to the highest pitch of rage; and, in the excess of her folly and brutality, endeavors, by loud, harsh threats, and the impetuous rattle of the cradle, to drown the infant's cries and to force him into slumber." For reasons such as these, the cradle began to pass from favor in the late eighteenth century and to be replaced eventually by the stationary crib in use today. Nonetheless, cradles continued to be used to some extent throughout the nineteenth century, for, as late as 1879, Mrs. Henry Ward Beecher warned young mothers to "allow no rocking or walking with the child. When every want is supplied the bed or crib is the best place for an infant in good health, and if this is acted upon from the beginning, the child will look for nothing else, it should never know that anything else can be had for the asking. It will not expect to be rocked to sleep: it will never know that it has lost anything by sleeping alone."[5]

Infants were not the only persons who enjoyed the calming motion of the cradle. A few surviving examples of the senility cradle (figure 7), a conventional rocking cradle large enough to accommodate an adult, suggest that a soothing rocking motion was considered beneficial for those aged persons who no longer took an active part in life. Presumably, the same benefits of cradles enjoyed by infants—sleep, exercise, and safety—pertained to the conditions of inactive senior citizens as well.

7. Adult rocking cradle of the early nineteenth century, probably made in New England. A few so-called "senility" cradles survive from the late eighteenth and early nineteenth centuries, an indication that the rocking motion was considered to be beneficial for those persons who were no longer mentally and physically active.

8. Butter fat is separated from milk by a repetitive motion. In this late eighteenth-century rocking churn, the traditional concept of churn with dasher was altered by mounting the churn on rockers.

From Stools to Chairs

Although the cradle was used in most homes prior to 1700, it swayed for many generations before someone was clever enough to see that the curved pieces which permitted the cradle to rock could be comfortably added to a chair. With the rocking chair in common use today, it is hard for most of us to understand why someone did not think of this ingenious application sooner. But the reason is relatively simple and lies within the history of the chair itself. The modern reader will be startled to learn that most people had not been sitting in a chair *of any kind* for very long before 1700.

Prior to the seventeenth century, arm chairs and back stools (known today as side chairs) were used primarily by heads of wealthy households. Most persons sat on chests or on plain and sometimes crude stools and benches. By the seventeenth century the quick and easily-made lathe-turned chair came into more common usage. And as the use of chairs became more and more common by the early eighteenth century, so also did improvements upon their comfort.

Throughout most of the history of the chair in the western world, chair backs were perpendicular. Although a straight back is surely preferable to the discomfort of sitting on a stool or bench, it is not as supportive as a curved or inclined chair back. Such is our level of comfort today that anyone who has ever sat in a dining or reception chair for any length of time knows how uneasy the perpendicular can be. Chair backs remained perpendicular throughout most of the seventeenth century, but by the end of the century the new "crown" chair, upholstered in cane, leather, or fabric, had a decidedly inclined back—a great improvement for prolonging the satisfaction of being seated. Once the art of off-center turning was mastered, these chairs were relatively easy to make in the high-style urban form. The plainer nonurban version remained perpendicular. The "crown" chair was revolutionary in its day and made an important impact on chair design. Subsequent improvements in the design of chair backs included the sensuous S-curve, introduced about 1720, which helped support the lumbar region of the back for greater comfort.

The desire to find an alternative to the perpendicular chair back is at the heart of the widespread practice of tilting a straight chair backwards on its two back legs. This entirely relaxed position continues to be quite popular as a nonformal sitting posture. Scorned in polite parlors and considered rude in formal dining situations, it is the very posture characteristic of men lounging on porches or in public bars or saloons. Comfort notwithstanding, etiquette books of the nineteenth century warned against tilting backwards since the practice was a sure sign of the ignorance of genteel behavior and of the proper elements of ceremonious social intercourse.

The same posture attained by tilting back in a chair is the position offered by the rocking chair, which by the very nature of its construction is tilted backwards. The rocking chair, however, is an infinitely better method of attaining this relaxed posture since there is much less danger of falling over backwards and no danger whatever of snapping off the fragile hind legs of stationary chairs. On the other hand, the rocking chair is a bit more cumbersome to move around, and is not as flexible as the non-rocking chair which can be both straight chair and tilting chair as needs change.

Easy Chairs

In the search for comfortable seating furniture, the easy chair, made in several varieties by the beginning of the eighteenth century, was an obvious improvement over the wooden chair because it was padded all over (figure 10). Valued by our wealthy ancestors and treasured by thir descendants, the easy chair has become a symbol of status, of comfort, and of the security of home and hearth itself. Today in England it is called a "grandfather's chair," a likely appellation when its original function of comfort for the infirm is understood. In America it is called a "wing chair," certainly a descriptive denotation. In the distant past, however, it was known universally as an easy chair. And how appropriate a name, for it conjures up thoughts of sinking in, dozing before the fire, reading a good book, relaxing, and taking life easy.

The easy chair probably originated in England and descended from a variety of upholstered couches and sleeping chairs that appeared during the sixteenth century among the furnishings made for the court. Sleeping chairs had reclining backs and some also had "eares" or wings attached to the sides of the backs. These wings were intended to keep draughts off the sitter so that he could enjoy the warmth of the fire. Some chairs with stationary backs were also equipped with upholstered wings for the same purpose.

Easy chairs were made in the closing years of the seventeenth century in the American colonies, although the earliest-known reference to one is in a New York City inventory of 1708. Since its introduction, the design of the easy chair has undergone few dramatic alterations in appearance. The ample proportions of conventional

9. *Mrs. Nicholas Salisbury* (Martha Saunders), painted by Christian Gullager in 1789. Seated in a large rose damask easy chair, and wearing an olive silk gown, Mrs. Salisbury (1704-1792) appears very much the way she must have looked to friends who visited with her in the friendly, intimate environment of her bed-chamber. Having just removed her spectacles, she is about to make an observation on what she has been reading. Inclusion of the easy chair in this portrait is a comment on her age, wealth, and perhaps physical condition. Gullager (1759-1826) has used Mrs. Salisbury's easy chair to great advantage. The decorative floral pattern gives the painting a pleasing originality in comparison to the plain or conventionally draped backgrounds typical of portraits of the period.

10. Easy chair made in America, 1780-1800. When easy chairs appear in eighteenth-century household inventories, they are usually located in bedrooms, where they served several functions. The allover padding provided for the comfort of elderly or infirm persons who had to remain seated for all or most of the day. The wings offered protection from cold draughts, which could be "totally excluded from the person asleep, by laying some kind of covering over the whole chair," as Thomas Sheraton recommended in his *Cabinet Dictionary* of 1803. Many easy chairs were also used as commodes, as in this example, one of the few extant which retains the extra frame for holding a chamber pot covered by the seat cushion.

examples had been achieved by about 1740, and, remarkably, they have changed very little since that time. The evolution of eighteenth-century taste, in fact, was reflected more in the shape and decoration of the legs than in the form itself; although even these variations are not at all helpful in distinguishing an easy chair of 1760 from one of 1785 or 1790. For example, "plain feet and knees," "claw feet," "claw feet and leaves on the knees," and "marlborough feet bases and brackets" were all options available to Philadelphia consumers in 1786. Generally, prices varied in relation to the amount of labor in-

volved in making the chair. Thus, in the 1780s and 1790s the style of legs an easy chair had depended more on the purchaser's pocketbook or personal taste than on prevailing fashions in other seating forms.[6]

Compared to the style-consciousness evident in side or arm chairs made during the same period, the easy chair emerges as a fairly conservative seating form in America, a fact which may be related to its functions, the persons who used it, and the rooms in which it was used. The conservatism of this upper-class furniture form has direct relevance to the rocking chair as well, for in many ways the rocking chair is an easy chair and fulfilled many of the same needs as the easy chair in the eighteenth century. Today, the easy chair decorates the best room in the house as it did in much of the nineteenth century. In the eighteenth and early nineteenth centuries, however, it was generally confined in use to bedchambers. Some writers have suggested that the easy chair was used primarily by the elderly or infirm because the allover padding of the chair increased the comfort of those who had to be seated all day. In his *Cabinet Dictionary* of 1803, for example, Thomas Sheraton illustrates a ''tub'' easy chair that is ''stuffed all over, and is intended for sick persons, being both easy and warm, for the side wings coming quite forward keep out the cold air, which may be totally excluded from the person asleep, by laying some kind of covering over the whole chair.'' The portrait of Mrs. Nicholas Salisbury painted by Christian Gullager in 1789 (figure 9) is one of the few eighteenth-century portraits with the sitter enthroned in an easy chair. Although his subject is advanced in age, Gullager gave Mrs. Salisbury a frame of soft decorative dignity. The easy chair was employed by the artist as a comment on both the age and social position of the sitter.[7]

In America, easy chairs may often have done double duty as commode chairs, although there are few surviving examples today with the frames in place which held the chamber pots. We do know that having a commode frame added to such chairs was certainly an option available to the consumer of the late eighteenth-century. Nonetheless, it is hard to accept the belief that *most* easy chairs were also used as commodes as some writers have claimed. Even owing for changes in social behavior and expectations between this century and the eighteenth, it is still difficult to believe that the aristocratic Mrs. Salisbury allowed her portrait to show her seated in a potty chair. While contemporary inventories clearly indicate that many easy chairs were kept in bedrooms, this fact alone does not necessarily mean that they were all used as commode chairs. In the eighteenth century, a wealthy person's bedchamber functioned as a private informal space, the inner sanctum of

11. A rocking horse such as this one is really a small rocking chair with a horse's head and extra long rockers in the front. Extant examples of this simple form were made in the nineteenth century, but reiterate that rocking horses and rocking chairs are cognates and suggest that cradles, rocking horses, and rocking chairs are all interrelated, with consideration for the child their common denominator.

22

the home, and was often used to entertain small groups of intimate friends. The parlor or salon, on the other hand, was the scene of formal entertainment for larger groups and was generally furnished with chairs, sofas, and couches for seating. In the homes of the very wealthy these would have been *en suite* in the latest fashion. Therefore, the easy chair, a seating form conducive to informal modes of behavior, was more suitable to the bedchamber. Furthermore, nineteenth-century books on home furnishing recommended using an easy chair in the bedroom in front of the fireplace to accommodate a lady during that uncertain period after rising between sleep and full wakefulness. The easy chair probably performed the same function for a lady of wealth in the eighteenth century, who with plenty of servants to take care of the household duties might indulge herself in a morning doze before the fire.

Thus the role of the easy chair was essential in the triumph of comfort that John Gloag, in *The Englishman's Chair* (1964), sees as the essence of the history of chair design since the seventeenth century:

The traditional association of chairs with an upright, dignified bearing was not overcome until the late seventeenth century when the easy chair was invented, and though nobody at the time suspected what this invention would do to good manners, it was the starting point of a slow but continuous decline of dignity. By increasing standards of comfort, chairmakers and upholsterers began to change posture through design, thus unwittingly changing the character of manners, which became less formal, easier, and in many ways happier, while dignity was relegated to royal and official functions. The gradual decay of elegance and the ultimate triumph of comfort are recorded by the chairs and seats in use throughout the Georgian and Victorian periods and by those we use today.

Early Rocking Chairs

Although the easy chair was essential to the development of comfort in elite seating furniture, the high cost of fabric upholstery meant that it was available only to wealthy urban buyers until well into the nineteenth century. The comfort improvements in chairs that affected a wider cross-section of the population occurred in the common side chair, the universal seating form after stools and benches were superseded as seating for the masses. The rocking chair was a product of the new attitudes toward seating furniture—the most important being a common understanding that chairs *could* be improved and that comfort was basic to the considerations of how to improve them.

The comfort attained from motion is obviously a large part of the attraction of the rocking chair—that gentle, repetitive, back and forth, over and over again motion. In the early eighteenth century, the motion that had put babies to sleep for many centuries suddenly became attractive to adults.

12. Child's rocking chair, New York or New Jersey, ealry eighteenth century. Little chairs such as this one, which were also often used for toilet training as well as for rocking, must have received hard wear as they were passed down from child to child. Even so, many more of these survive than do adult rocking chairs of the same period, a fact possibly indicating that children's rockers were more numerous or that they were more highly treasured by descendants. Painted decoration was added to the back about 1800 when someone felt that this chair should be preserved. The delicately painted shield held by a pink ribbon and flanked by floral branches on the back is embellished with "LH" for a child who used this chair in the mid-eighteenth century.

Although the word "rocker" has several meanings today—all of them to some extent referring to a characteristic back and forth motion—the earliest use of "rocker" in the English language occurred in the fifteenth century in reference to the nurse or attendant responsible for rocking the cradle. A variant meaning of "rocker" was used in the eighteenth century to describe an orator who put others to sleep. Thus, the primary association of the rocking motion with the cradle, and of monotony and repetition as inducements to sleep, is quite clear.

Beyond monotony and repetition, however, motion is important for comfort because of physiological reasons which our ancestors may or may not have consciously understood. One method of attaining relaxation is to shift the position of the body in relation to the earth's gravity. The motion of the rocking chair, therefore, offers a convenient vehicle for obtaining such a shift and so contributes to the comfort of the sitter.

Because the attainment of comfort through the rocking motion was basically an informal mode of behavior, eighteenth-century rocking chairs that survive, whether they started life with rockers or not, are generally of the informal or common variety—slatbacks, bannister backs, and Windsors—with but few exceptions. There were as well in the eighteenth century three types of informal chairs thought suitable to receive rockers—the

13. The small armless rocking chair with seat relatively close to the floor is basically a work chair that evolved particularly from the nurse chair, or more generally from the side chair. In nineteenth-century furniture catalogues, it is often referred to as a ''nurse rocker,'' ''sewing rocker,'' or ''ladies' rocker,'' suggesting that it was used by women for housekeeping chores that could be performed sitting down in comfort. Except for the Boston rocker near the windows and the lantern above, this interior, signed by Edward Hill and dated 1885, might have been painted as early as 1790.

14. *Above:* Rocking armchair, Delaware River Valley, 1785-1815. Rockers were added with screws to the worn legs of this armchair after it had been used for some time. Before its conversion, the chair may well have been part of a set of chairs for the parlor-dining room. As a chair passed from fashion, its usefulness could be extended by adding rockers and moving it to a second floor bedchamber or back porch for less formal seating.

15. Invalids were among the most frequent occupants of the early rocking chair. In this newspaper woodcut of the Civil War period, the rocking chair and crutches provide convenient symbols for the physical condition of the sick and wounded. "The old hero of Gettysburg" was drawn from a photograph by Timothy O'Sullivan and appeared in *Harper's Weekly* for August 22, 1863.

child's chair, the nurse chair, and the common ladder-back or Windsor arm chair. The child's chair was probably the first type to become a rocking chair. The transference of rockers from cradle to chair was a thoughtful way of extending the pleasure of rocking as a baby to rocking as a child. With its origin in the mid-seventeenth century, the rocking horse seems to be the perfect bridge between cradle and child's rocker. Early nineteenth-century rocking horses that are literally elaborate rocking chairs confirm that these are cognate forms (figure 11). In addition, there are eighteenth-century children's rocking chairs of board construction which are low to the ground with very high backs and small wings ending in suggestive arms, similar to plastic tub-like baby carriers in use today (figure 12). Several of these board rocking chairs served double duty as potty chairs as well. With a cushion to cover the hole when not in use, these little chairs easily provided

a dual-purpose furniture form, so useful in houses that were short on space. There are few persons who do not marvel at the odd combination of functions embodied in a rocking potty chair.

A second form of chair readily suitable for the addition of rockers was the nurse chair, a small scale, low-seated piece of furniture (figure 13). The nurse chair was useful to the child's nurse or mother in at least two ways: it allowed her to be in a more convenient position for rocking the cradle with her foot, and the posture produced by sitting lower formed a cozier lap in which to hold a baby for nursing or other purposes. In one sense, the nurse rocker extends the child's pleasures from rocking alone in a cradle to rocking when held by another human being in a chair. In fact, when a child is held and rocked in a rocking chair, the child moves in the same side-to-side motion as in a typical cradle, while the caretaker moves in the back-to-front motion associated with the rocking

16. Invalid chair, New England, 1760-1800. The posture of a nonambulatory invalid or aged person who must remain seated for most or all of the day is more restful if his back does not have to be perpendicular. Although this chair does not rock, the manner in which the chair back is inclined suggests the same angle normally attained by the rocking chair's construction, and reiterates as well that the rocking chair is a comfortable seating form for immobile persons. Here the inclination is contrived to be stable, supported by two extra legs at the rear. In the mid-nineteenth century, patents were granted for chairs that rocked, rolled, and reclined.

17. Details of this rocking chair made between 1750 and 1800 recommend it as one of the grandest slat-back rocking chairs to survive from the Delaware Valley. This six shaped slats, boldy turned front stretcher, double-scoring on the finials and balusters of the front posts, and extra flourish to the undercut arms suggest the hand of an especially artful craftsman. These same details are also the defining characteristics of eighteenth- and early nineteenth-century common chairs made in the Delaware River Valley bounded by Pennsylvania, New Jersey, and Delaware. The front curl on the rockers, a decorative safety feature to keep the chair from rocking all the way forward, is occasionally found on cradles as well.

chair. The child's enjoyment is enhanced, and pleasure is also afforded to the other human being, usually female.

The common arm chair is a third informal chair type that can have rockers. The pleasures, advantages, and tranquility associated with rocking children for so many centuries were apparently perceived to be equally beneficial to adults. But would these early rockers have been meant for adults of all ages, and for men as well as for women? Although eighteenth-century rocking arm chairs survive, it is doubtful that vigorous young or middle-aged men would have found them as attractive as, for instance, the "La-Z-Boy" rocker-recliner is to Joe Namath today. Visual evidence of the use of rocking chairs in the nineteenth-century home indicates that, unless they were invalid or elderly, men rarely used rocking chairs to any great extent until perhaps the mid-nineteenth century. Rather, in the eighteenth and early nineteenth centuries rocking arm chairs were more a part of senior adulthood, of retirement from the hardest labors of life (figure

15). Thus the interest in providing the aged with a relaxing place to sit was an impetus to move rockers from cradles to chairs. In this context, easy chairs and rocking chairs become intwined. In the nineteenth century, in fact, the term "easy chair" was occasionally used to denote a rocking chair. Despite the fact that easy chairs were often used by the elderly, they were far too expensive for most pocketbooks. Many of the easy chair's benefits, however, could be obtained simply and cheaply by adding rockers to a favorite straight chair.

Although the rocking chair is associated primarily with children and older persons in pictorial evidence of the past—both in real transcriptions from life and in depictions symbolic of home, happiness, and harmony—others used and enjoyed rocking chairs, too. By the second quarter of the nineteenth century, most Americans were familiar with the rocking chair and probably used one during all periods of life—if not daily, at least occasionally.

18. *Right:* Writing-arm Windsor chairs do not often appear with rockers, but they do survive as made in this manner originally or converted at a later date. In 1832, William Beesley, a chairmaker in Salem, New Jersey, charged $1.50 to alter a chair by the addition of rockers and "writing bord."

19. Rocking roundabout chair, probably made in New Jersey about 1800. This ingenious addition of rockers to a roundabout chair is most unusual. Although the rockers are not original, they add greatly to the comfort of the chair and the ease with which the chair can be tilted back for lounging.

Is This Rocking Chair Original?

However the rocking chair developed, it was an informal piece of furniture in the eighteenth century and, as such, was treated in a very informal way. No one paid close attention to its design. It was simply a chair that rocked. It was a chair with rockers added. And whether the chair had its rockers added the day it was made, or several years afterward, made almost no difference in the design of the chair. This is why it is so difficult to distinguish between the chair made *originally* as a rocking chair and the one made as a chair with rockers put on some time after its manufacture. Not until the nineteenth century did chairmakers begin to think of the rocking chair as a distinct seating form which could be made more comfortable, as well as more popular, with a little concerted consciousness of its design.

For some connoisseurs, the fact that a chair was made to rock after its original manufacture detracts from its value. Once it is determined that a chair did not rock originally, the rockers are removed by the fastidious owner and the notches previously cut into the legs to accommodate rockers are filled in. To the American mind there is honor in the concept of originality—that is, the first is best or most important. Wallace Nutting in 1917 voiced his generation's attitude when he noted that "As it is no longer good form to rock, and for that matter never could have been [Nutting was a very formal person], we need not grieve over the false Windsor rocker, except to regret that so many thousand perfectly good Windsors have been spoiled by adding rockers."[8]

On the other hand, there are many persons today—scholars, connoisseurs, and collectors alike—who feel that an object should reflect its history of use. Antiques dealers speak of "honest wear" in referring to a nicked and gouged surface of paint or varnish, or the small chip out of the edge of an historical blue Staffordshire plate. This opinion can easily be turned toward converted chairs. In many cases it really does not matter which came first, the rocker or the chair. The importance of such a chair may lie in what it was originally, as well as in the fact that it was later made to rock—in the fact that someone, somewhere in the history of the particular chair, wanted to use it for rocking.

There is abundant evidence in chairmakers' account books to indicate that chairs often received

20. When his *Colonial Furniture in America* was published in 1913, Luke Vincent Lockwood regarded this example as "the earliest rocking chair" that he had found. The chair, made about 1700, is distinguished by the fact that the bottom of the rear legs were left as blocks when the posts were turned, an indication that the chair was originally intended to receive rockers, or perhaps wheels.

rockers at some time after their manufacture (figure 14). Even as late as the first quarter of the nineteenth century, nonurban chairmakers, such as William Beesley who worked in southern New Jersey about 1825-35, made rocking chairs occasionally as called for and continued to add rockers to existing chairs as their eighteenth-century predecessors had done. The latter practice undoubtedly persisted because it was more economical to have rockers added than to have a rocking chair newly made. In 1828, Beesley charged $3.50 to make a rocking chair, but only 50¢ to convert an existing chair. Thus the problem in determining originality of rocker attachment becomes even more complex. Was the artifact made as a rocking chair, or was it converted to that use at a later date? Or was it fabricated in the back of a dealer's shop the day before yesterday?[9]

Some writers on the subject have insisted that the length and shape of rockers are the primary clues to date of manufacture. Rockers that extend equidistantly in both directions from the chair legs are considered earlier than rockers that extend farther to the rear. Boldly-shaped rockers with good height are considered earlier than the thinner, more gracefully-defined rockers. In this scheme, short boldly shaped rockers on an early chair would suggest that it was made originally as a rocking chair, whereas narrow rockers extending a greater distance behind the legs of an early chair would indicate a later conversion. Although this interpretation may have some validity, it does not allow for individual variation. Today, for example, the Tell City Chair Company manufactures a rocking chair for "less active" people. It is fitted with short rockers so that it does not pitch back in a way that older people or invalids would consider disconcertingly uncomfortable. The same type of adaptation could have easily been used in the eighteenth and nineteenth centuries.

While these gross visual characteristics may give the observer an initial impression of the age of a rocking chair, they are certainly not the only signs to look for. The number and placement of stretchers has also been noted as an important clue in determining the legitimacy of the rockers. One stretcher per side, placed equidistantly between seat rail and rocker, would indicate an original rocking chair. Two stretchers on the sides, placed very close to the rocker, would suggest a later conversion, because the length of the chair legs would have had to be cut down in order to accommodate the extra height of rockers. Again, looks can be deceiving. The same Tell City Chair Company senior citizen's rocker has an extra high seat to make it easier to get in and out of. A footstool can be used to elevate the feet to the proper level once seated. Since early rocking chairs were usually made to order, the same accommodation may well have been executed by an obliging chairmaker in the eighteenth century. Smaller details of construction must be inspected to be certain that these characteristics are true indicators of the chair's original condition. Of course, one of the easiest ways to tell if the chair was made initially as a rocker is to determine if the ends of the legs were left purposely broader to accept rockers, as in the early rocking chair in figure 20. Here the ends of the back legs were left as blocks to provide a sturdy connection for the rockers.

Inspection of paint layers on early rocking chairs may aid in the detection of original rockers. Because most eighteenth-century rocking chairs were variations on common chairs made of several types of woods, those that are found today were painted at the time of manufacture. Slatback, bannister-back, and Windsor chairs were constructed from a variety of woods, each chosen for its distinguishing characteristics—soft, easily-worked pine or tulip made good seats, the flexible ash or hickory made excellent spindles and bowed

Windsor chairs were popularly made into rockers in the late eighteenth and early nineteenth centuries. Use of "combs" on Windsor rocking chairs and settees made the backs higher and more comfortable for rocking. Comfort was further enhanced by the use of cushions for seat and back.

21. *Left:* Rocking chair, possibly made in New England, 1775-1810.

22. Rocking chair branded A: HAGGET, CHARLESTOWN, c. 1800.

23. Rocking settee, probably made in New England, 1790-1815.

backs, the hard and durable maple was appropriate for long-lasting legs because it could also be easily turned on a lathe. Eighteenth-century taste valued unity over the beauty of natural wood in chairs made of several woods, so common chairs were ordinarily painted. When examining an eighteenth-century rocking chair with original paint, either exposed or under one or more later paint layers, care should be taken to determine whether the paint on chair and rockers match. For example, if a rocking chair is painted grey over black over green, all three layers should appear on the rockers as well as on the chair if the piece of furniture was originally made to be a rocking chair. On the other hand, if the chair's original green layer does not appear on the rockers, then one might suspect that

33

24. Acadian rocking chair of about 1810. Plainly elegant rocking chairs made by Acadian furniture craftsmen in Nova Scotia and New Brunswick are the most distinctive type of Canadian rocking chairs which tend otherwise to be in the conventional American patterns. The overall characteristic which distinguishes the Acadian examples is that they are not turned chairs. Legs, posts, and often stretchers are square or rectangular rather than round. Acadian chair backs are composed of slats and splats, in combination on the best examples, rather than of spindles. When arms are employed, they are close to the seat. Often a second stretcher is used just below the line of the seat.

they were added some time after the date of manufacture—*although it could still be an original rocking chair.* The first rockers, after all, might have been replaced sometime shortly before the chair was painted black. This would certainly confound the diagnosis if it were based on the analysis of paint layers alone.

Rockers could have been added to a chair in several ways: by doweling the legs into the rockers from above, by placing the rockers into slots cut into the center of the legs, or by placing the rockers into notches made on the outside or inside of the legs. When chair legs have been doweled into the rockers, determination of legitimacy may have to be based on analysis of paint layers. Doweled ends that have been whittled to achieve their shape are extremely suspicious because the chairmaker would normally turn the dowel on the lathe when he shaped the rest of the leg. If the rockers can be removed, lathe chuck marks should show on the ends of the chair legs.

When rockers have been attached into slots or notches, a close look at details of the construction process can be extremely revealing. A rule that is commonly repeated states that wooden pins or pegs were used to join rockers to chair legs prior to 1830; after that period screws generally secured the joint. Here again, however, the connoisseur can be stymied. An authentic rocking chair of the late eighteenth century may have had its first set of rockers re-attached with screws in the 1850s. On the other hand, someone wishing to enhance an otherwise plain little nurse chair, might have added rockers to its worn-down legs by using pegs. The continued use of traditional furniture-making techniques by some chairmakers even into the twentieth century contradicts this too-easy rule.

The amount of wear on the bottoms of rockers can be an indication of how recently they have been added. This wear will tell the observer whether or not the rockers were used on the chair for a long period of time, but will not in and of itself reveal if the chair was originally a rocking chair.

All the evidence of the chair's manufacture, use, and repair must be taken into account, for there are no easy rules to use in determining the age and originality of rockers on informal chairs. And after all of the above has been taken into consideration, there is one final and all-important judgment to make—is it a successful rocking chair? Does it satisfy the requirements of being a useful rocking chair? Is it quiet and soothing, a chair for relaxation and refreshment? It it easy and comfortable?

Although some of the rocking chair's earliest history must be based on conjecture and inference, the wealth of material available for an understanding of its place in the nineteenth century brings our knowledge of this artifact into focus. If the eighteenth century is a time of relative darkness in our understanding of the rocking chair's development, the nineteenth century is a period which is crystal clear. There is a good deal of evidence for the use and manufacture of rocking chairs in the later century—in terms of the words that were written about them, the greater frequency with which they appear in pictures, and the enormous numbers of them which survive. The story, as we shall see in the chapter that follows, becomes one of a popular furniture form that could be adapted to nearly every fashion, pocketbook, individual preference, or purpose.

25. Black striping on the legs, stretchers, and spindles of this bronze-stenciled yellow child's rocking chair is meant to imitate the bamboo turnings of many chairs of slightly earlier date. Although the side stretchers are close to the rockers on this example, the rockers are original to the chair.

2.
"These Wooden Narcotics"

Many writers have speculated on whether rocking chairs originated in England or in America. Jane Toller's assertion in 1973 that "rocking chairs have been used in the British Isles ever since chairs replaced stools, and [that] it must have been the early immigrant cabinet-makers from Britain who started the fashion in America" is a glib pronouncement that has no substantiation in fact. John Gloag, who has written a great deal on English furniture, hedges by saying that while the rocking chair may have been invented in America, an early eighteenth-century origin "has been claimed for Lancashire." In spite of these British longings for primacy, the reactions of nineteenth-century travelers to the rocking chair's common appearance in America and to its lack of use in Britain affirm that the rocking chair had its origins in the colonies rather than in the mother country. Indeed, commentators much closer to the source than we are today emphatically distinguished the rocking chair as an American invention.[1]

A contributor to *The Northern Galaxy* (Middletown, Vermont) of December 11, 1844, noticed "in a recent London paper...American Rocking Chairs, in which the comfort and luxurious ease of these wooden narcotics are most elaborately delineated. New to us is it, that the rocking chair is of exclusive American contrivance and use, and yet so it is." During the same period that this anonymous chronicler enlightened his American readers on their country's contribution to comfort, Herman Humphrey, the president of Amherst College, recorded his observations of the Englishman's home from first-hand experience.

I have said, that everything in a respectable English domicile is exceedingly comfortable. But I ought, perhaps to add, that when I had been in the country three or four months, a friend said to me one day, "Do you notice that the English have no *rocking chairs*?" The question, I confess, had never occurred to me till that moment; but I could not recollect that I had seen one, anywhere. Afterwards, I met with two or three, I believe, but they were *Americanisms*; and though it was confessed that they were a very taking Yankee contrivance for loungers, I could not perceive that there was any prospect of their gaining much favor with our staid and upright kindred in the "Father Land." If they should, however, may we not expect to hear it stoutly maintained, that they are a *British invention*?[2]

Taken together, these two observations effectively dismiss any notion that rocking chairs were enjoyed in England before they became popular in America. Indeed, in the early nineteenth century, the English generally regarded rocking in chairs as a despicably "American" preoccupation. In a published account of her visit to America (1835), Frances Anne Butler described the use of rocking chairs on the steamer *Charles Carroll*:

I went below for a few minutes, but found, as usual, the atmosphere of the cabin perfectly intolerable. The ladies' cabin, in winter, on board one of these large steamers, is a right curious sight. 'T is generally crammed to suffocation with women, *strewn* in every direction. The greater number cuddle round a stove, the heat of which alone would make the atmosphere unbreathable. Others sit lazily in a species of rocking-chair,—which is found wherever Americans sit down,—cradling themselves backwards and forwards, with a lazy, lounging, sleeping air, that makes me long to make them get up and walk.

In the same vein, the famous English traveler Harriet Martineau recorded her journey between Stockbridge, Massachusetts, and Albany, New York, in 1838:

> In these small inns the disagreeable practice of rocking in the chair is seen in its excess. In the inn parlors are three or four rocking chairs in which sit ladies who are vibrating in different directions and at various velocities, so as to try the head of a stranger...How this lazy and ungraceful indulgence ever became general, I cannot imagine; but the nation seems wedded to it, that I see little chance of its being forsaken. When American ladies come to live in Europe, they sometimes send home for a rocking chair. A common wedding present is a rocking chair. A beloved pastor has every room in his house furnished with a rocking chair by his grateful and devoted people.[3]

Despite their rather snobbish attitude towards rocking, these two observant Englishwomen offer us some important insights into the use of rocking chairs in early nineteenth-century America. Since both observations are of ladies rocking, it is clear that the rocking chair continued to be more closely associated with women than with men. Its appropriateness as a wedding gift speaks of the rocking chair's importance in the home as a woman's work chair. Its use by the clergyman is probably related to his less than vigorous life-style. Mindful of his comfort, the "grateful and devoted people"

who saw to it "that every room in his house [was] furnished with a rocking chair" were no doubt reminding him as well that his work required a good deal more meditation than that of the craftsman, tradesman, farmer, or laborer. If knowledge of the rocking chair's origins and use in the eighteenth century is difficult to grasp with any certainty, there is no doubt of its widespread use by the early nineteenth century. It was apparently ubiquitous "wherever Americans sit down," as Miss Butler put it. Nor is there any doubt of its comfortable, addictive qualities since, as Miss Martineau observed, "when American ladies come to live in Europe, they sometimes send home for a rocking chair."

Although most English commentators considered rocking a distasteful pastime, there were those who recognized the ingenuity and resourcefulness inherent in this American invention. In his treatise on *The Americans in their Moral, Social, and Political Relations* (1837), Francis J. Grund expressed a true regard for the rocking chair as an example of the inquiring and practical American mind, traits that were soon to become evident to surprised Europeans at the Great Exhibition of 1851 in London:

> Furniture is made in Philadelphia, Boston, and New York, much better than in any part of the continent of Europe, Paris itself not excepted; and the New England "rocking-chairs," the *ne plus ultra* of all comforts in the shape of furniture, have acquired an European reputation. It is not so much the elegance as the excellent adaptation to the purpose for which they are intended, which distinguishes every article manufactured in the United States. One sees at once that the maker must have been a thinking creature, who understood all the time what he was about, and left nothing undone which could materially improve the usefulness of his handicraft.

When in 1838 James Frewin recorded for the London *Architectural Magazine* his observations on the rocking chairs he saw in St. Louis, his language was more matter-of-fact. "In America," he wrote "it is considered a compliment to give the stranger the rocking-chair as a seat; and when there is more than one kind in the house, the stranger is always presented with the best."[4]

26. A fancy painted rocking chair provides a seat for this little girl painted in the United States by an unknown artist, about 1840.

27. Stoneware jug with painted vignette, American, c. 1830. Two men enjoy a draught from "The Little Brown Jug" as they toast each other near a cooking stove. Sitting backwards in an armless rocking chair is a position guaranteed to enhance the disorienting effects of alcohol.

The Rocker in Art

If rocking chairs were a socially acceptable and generally popular form of seating furniture in America as these accounts indicate, then we should expect to find them often portrayed in visual records. The fact is, however, that rocking chairs are not included in pictures from the past as often as are side chairs or even arm chairs. If we did not already know better, this fact alone might suggest that rocking chairs were not a popular seating form.

No eighteenth-century pictures have been found that include rocking chairs. This is not so surprising since, as we've already seen, the form was not widely used for seating until the second quarter of the nineteenth century. Approximately three-quarters of the nineteenth-century portraits which depict the sitter in a rocking chair are of children or of old persons. One might conclude that rocking chairs were used only by these two age groups or that rocking chairs were too infor-

28. John and Abigail Montgomery, recorded by Joseph H. Davis in 1836, relax in the later years of their very productive lives. They are shown in a colorful, comfortable middle-class interior of the period, surrounded by some of the fruits of their labors—apples from their orchard on the decoratively painted table and a relatively expensive ingrain carpet on the floor. They are respectable, literate, and religious people. Their painted Windsor-type rocking chairs are just rewards for their lives of virtue and hard work.

mal to be included in portraiture. But these deductions alone, despite their logic, do not reveal the entire story.

If rocking chairs were principally associated with children and the aged, then it would have been inappropriate for healthy adults to be pictured in them, even if those same persons habitually used rocking chairs every day. Even today, most persons having their portraits taken at home by professional painters or photographers would probably not choose to be recorded in a rocking chair unless it were an important element in their lives. An arm chair, easy chair, or sofa would typically be considered more appropriate for the record. Candid home photographs taken by Uncle Charlie, on the other hand, are quite different. Propriety is not an important element of this informal genre. Unfortunately, this type of photography was quite rare until the later nineteenth century because of the long exposure times and

41

complicated equipment that were necessary before the perfection of the portable roll-film camera. From the time the daguerreotype was invented in the late 1830s, until George Eastman offered the first mail-order film developing in 1888, professional photographers were about the only persons who could cope with photographic processing. Portraits, therefore, generally show the formal or public side of the sitter, not those thoughtful, end-of-the-day or quiet evening-paper moments when the rocking chair is most comfortable—which is why so few eighteenth- and early-nineteenth-century portraits include rocking chairs. Healthy vigorous adults want to show their best side, so to speak, but children can be allowed to be children and old people can be comfortable—even in portraiture. By the early nineteenth century, childhood was considered a special, informal, and enjoyable period in a middle-class person's life, while old age was a time to relax and rest after a busy and productive

life. Both of these elements—unbridled enjoyment and restful relaxation—are embodied in the rocking chair.

The watercolors, paintings, prints, and silhouettes shown throughout this chapter emphasize many conclusions drawn from the written record of the same period. A man appears in a rocking chair in only one of the portraits, a painting by Joseph Davis (figure 28). From the cane he holds and his age of 56, it is clear that he is no longer a vigorous man. His top hat, the open Bible, and the dog at his feet suggest that he is a successful, religious, and respected person. He and his wife enjoy the comforts attained by having worked hard during their lives.

Jacob Maentel and Deborah Goldsmith have drawn two successful families as well, yet both families are much younger than the Montgomerys in Davis's portrait. In Maentel's watercolor of an unidentified family (figure 29) the two youngest sisters appear to rock before our very eyes, while

29. *Opposite:* The young children in the foreground of Jacob Maentel's early nineteenth-century *Family Portrait* seem to be rocking even now in striking contrast to the formally stiff posture of the other family members. Maentel achieved the effect of motion in the rocking chairs by magnifying the shape of the rockers beyond what would have been their normal proportions. Comparison with a rocking chair of the same type and period in figure 25 indicates the extent of the exaggeration. The type of chair each member of the family sat in for this portrait was not an arbitrary choice—father has an armchair, mother and the three older children sit in side chairs. Seating the two younger children in rocking chairs was a device to keep them smaller and in the foreground.

30. Deborah Goldsmith's (1803-1836) close attention to detail in this portrait of the Talcott family of Hamilton, New York, dated March 16, 1832, indicates that the characteristics of the elder woman are not accidental. Her black costume and close-fitting cap, the eyeglasses and prayer book clasped in her lap, and her rocking chair all identify her advanced age and set her apart from the young couple.

31. Auguste Edouart created a typical "conversation piece" in this *Family Silhouette* dated 1842—each member of the family has individuality and at the same time is engaged in an activity with another member of the family. Mother and father converse at the center of the composition, flanked by their children who entertain their grandmothers at either side of the picture. We are looking into an upper-class urban parlor decorated in the late-classical style. Only an upholstered rocking chair could appear in such a fashionable and formal room during this period.

the rest of the family is shown in stiffly formal poses in surprising contrast to the vividly-patterned floor and walls. *The Talcott Family* by Deborah Goldsmith (figure 30) is a portrait which spans three generations. The older woman is distinguished from the younger by her dark costume, closely-covering bonnet, eyeglasses, preoccupation with religion (the prayer book on her lap) rather than with young children, and of course her rocking chair. Goldsmith's close attention to detail in the floor and wall coverings, furniture, and costumes affirms that the distinctions which appear between the two women are not accidental.

In his group silhouette of 1842 (figure 31), Auguste Edouart introduces a family different in terms of wealth, location, and taste, but a family in which distinctions of sex and age are not dissimilar from those of the other three families. The family is in the parlor of an urban home decorated in the fashionable late-Empire taste, and appropriately, grandmother is seated in an upholstered rocker rather than in one of the Windsor-derived varieties seen in the other portraits. Although the figures are depicted only in the details of their silhouettes, the background of the room and its furnishings show a similar attention to detail even down to the lamp's reflection in the pier mirror and the sea shells on the lower shelf of the pier table.

The portrait of Jane Rebecca Griffith (figure 34), attributed to Oliver T. Eddy, is of the same period as Edouart's silhouetted family. In fact, the details of the room—the geometric carpet, heavy late-Empire furniture, and classically plain walls accented only by columns—are very similar. Even

32. *Mrs. John Maynard Davis* (Mary Elizabeth Moncrieff), 1770-1847, signed by Samuel Metford, c. 1840. Mrs. Davis was over seventy years of age when Samuel Metford cut her silhouette. Rocking was (and is still) considered an excellent form of indoor exercise for the elderly because a beneficial effect on the circulation is obtained with a minimum of effort. Use of a footstool keeps the knees elevated. Although she may have been confined to her home at such advanced age, Mrs. Davis obviously kept active in her rocking chair while she watched over the bustle of the harbor at Charleston, South Carolina.

the upholstered rocking chair is of the same type. But the subject is very different and represents an exception to the generalization that rocking chairs in portraiture are appropriate only for children and grandparents. In contrast to the subjects of other portraits, Jane Griffith does not sit in the rocking chair. Is she thinking of sitting in it or is she thinking of someone, now gone, who used to sit in it—a parent, grandparent, fiancé, spouse? Is this perhaps a posthumous portrait—was she sitting in it before her own death at an early age after a long illness which confined her to the chair? Or did she merely have her portrait painted while standing next to her favorite chair? Whatever the reason, the portrait would be unusual even if she were leaning against a straight chair.

Genre painting of this early period reveals another side to the rocking chair story, although it seems to offer even fewer scenes with rocking chairs than do portraits. Margarita Münch's birth and baptismal certificate (1826) is one of the earliest depictions of a rocking chair in any media (figure 35). Certificate illumination was a formalized art, practiced in strongly German groups in Pennsylvania and Virginia. These certificates rarely show the urge for genre seen in the four corner vignettes of Carl Münch's work. More than a family frozen at a single time in space, the Münches reveal several aspects of their very comfortable lives together in and around their substantial farm, relaxing, harvesting, and working indoors. In the lower left, mother relaxes in a rocking chair beneath a bower and displays a small bird for her young son. The continued association of rocking chairs with motherhood is also seen in John Warner Barber's wood-engraving of a parlor by night (figure 36). The mother with a cap is seated in an armless rocking chair, the type suitable for work, as she instructs her daughters from a book. The basket near one daughter suggests that they have been sewing.

33. *Chief Justice John Marshall and Mary Ambler Marshall*, by S. M. Gerry, Richmond, Virginia, April 10, 1830. The Marshalls face each other in silhouette, seated in common chairs of the period. While Mrs. Marshall has settled comfortably into a plain rocking chair, possibly a bow-back Windsor type covered to make it softer for long periods of sitting, Chief Justice Marshall holds a book in a cane-back arm chair. By 1830 the Marshalls were well advanced in age (he was seventy-five years old) and certainly deserved some time to relax.

34. *Jane Rebecca Griffith*, attributed to Oliver T. Eddy, c. 1840. Miss Griffith's quiet contemplative gaze over the back of a rocking chair in a fashionable late-classical parlor suggests a tragedy in her life since women of her age were rarely associated with rocking chairs during this period. The upholstered Grecian rocking chair on which she leans is an excellent example of what was a very popular type by the mid-nineteenth century. It is really an open-arm chair with rockers. The defining characteristics of the type are its high contour back and jigsaw-cut scrolled arm terminals. More expensive models had arm terminals elaborately carved with swans, double scrolls, eagles, and other classical devices.

35. *Above:* Illuminated certificate made for Margareta Münch by Carl Münch, in Penns Township, Northumberland County, Pennsylvania, in 1826. Although the illumination of birth, baptismal, confirmation, and wedding certificates was commonly practiced among German groups living in Pennsylvania and Virginia, few show the originality and urge to record scenes of everyday life evident in this delightfully decorative example. The vignette at the lower left shows a young mother in a rocker.

36. The armless chair on short rockers in this illustration by John Warner Barber is a woman's work chair. The angle of the back provides a restful position while the short rockers give the chair just enough motion to keep the sitter's legs from losing their circulation during such tedious chores as sewing and mending, which require long periods of sitting. The rhythmic rocking sets the pace, like a metronome, for repetitive work motions.

37. Rocking armchair made by Nathaniel Dominy V at East Hampton, Long Island, 1804-1830. Although the account books of the Dominy family date from 1766-1847, the two rocking chairs made in 1804 for John Lyon Gardiner, their wealthiest client, are the first rockers to appear in their records. Twelve rocking chairs were produced by 1830, but there is no indication that Dominy ever added rockers to existing chairs. This four-slat-back half-arm chair form is typical of the rocking chairs made on Long Island and along the coast of Connecticut.

The Market Expands

In addition to their value as documents of customs and taste, these paintings, drawings, and prints also show the varieties of rocking chairs in use during the first half of the nineteenth century. Certainly by the period of the new republic the rocking chair had become a much more generally used and popular seating form. Perhaps word about the ease and comfort of the rocking chair spread rapidly during the Revolutionary War as men from diverse areas became acquainted with each other and traded ideas. Men from villages where the rocking chair was unknown would certainly have joined arms with men from villages where rocking was accepted. And, sadly, many more wounded and sickly men would have had occasion to find the rocking chair of use and comfort when they returned home from battle.

No one really knows if demand creates supply or whether supply creates demand, but, in any case, chairmakers began to produce and advertise more rocking chairs by 1800. Many nonurban chairmakers continued well into the nineteenth century to add rockers to existing chairs, as did William Beesley of Salem, New Jersey. On the other hand, craftsmen serving similarly rural populations apparently never had to perform that task because their customers ordered rocking chairs made new. One such craftsman, Nathaniel Dominy V, made a total of twelve rocking chairs between 1804 and 1830 for his customers in East Hampton, Long Island (figure 37). None of the rockers were conversions from regular chairs. In comparison to the prices recorded for the various types of chairs the Dominy family made, these four-slat half-arm rocking chairs were among the more expensive chairs produced.[5]

While Beesley and the Dominys represent craftsmen who made a living at their trade, there were other chairmakers who worked on a part-time basis. Jesse Esbin of East Goshen Township in Chester County, Pennsylvania, for example, recorded only thirty-seven pieces of furniture sold during the thirteen years for which his account book survives (1824-42). Sixteen of this total, nearly half, were rocking chairs for which he charged $1.50 to $2.00 each. These were probably a plain slat-back variety with a rush seat.[6]

Local craftsmen like Beesley, Esbin, and the Dominys generally operated their businesses on an "order" basis, making chairs as they were required by their customers. This type of business operation was in strong contrast to the methods used by merchant-chairmakers who kept a well-stocked salesroom in or near their shops. They also employed skilled, unskilled, and apprentice labor, unlike the local chairmaker who could meet his demand with fewer hands. Joseph Jones, a chairmaker in West Chester, Pennsylvania, from 1817-1846, is an example of the merchant-craftsman. His November 7, 1821, advertisement in West Chester's *Village Record* indicates that he had "on hand a general assortment of Fancy Chairs, Settees, Writing Chairs, Chamber Chairs, Rocking Chairs, Rush Bottom Chairs, &c., &c.

38. A rocking chair of uncoventional design and oversized proportions (64" x 28" x 26"), this example was intended to draw attention to the New England chairmaking firm which displayed it as a trade sign on its roof during the second quarter of the nineteenth century.

39. Rocking armchair attributed to John Foreman, Jr., Jennersville, Chester County, Pennsylvania, 1825-50. Like his father, John Foreman, Jr. (1801-1879) was a chairmaker and probably served a fairly local clientele familiar with his work. Since he did not advertise in local newspapers or label his chairs, his business was probably as large as it needed to be to satisfy him, or at least he had no pretensions to make more chairs than met the needs of his local community. While this chair has the proportions of the popular large Boston rocker—especially noticeable in the high back—its details of construction and decoration link it more closely in appearance to common chairs with slat backs and thumb-molded stiles. The regular chair-back height has been extended to provide enough support for the head in leaning back to rock.

finished in the handsomest and most fashionable manner of the best materials and workmanship." Jones may also have been retailing other makers' chairs since he advertised in 1836 that he had "more than 50 dozen on Hand! ...ready for the spring sale; among them [were] curled maple fancy Chairs with cane and rush seats; some rockered with cane backs."[7]

Labeling is another business practice more characteristic of the merchant-chairmaker than the local chairmaker, whose clientele become familiar with his work and do not need to be reminded of who the best chairmaker in the area is because he is often the only one in the area. John Foreman, Jr., of West Fallowfield Township in Chester County did not advertise in area newspapers, but his distinctive chairs must have been quite recognizable to the people he served (figure 39). While a label, in and of itself, can enhance the value of a rocking chair to some degree, a label represents a type of business practice; it does not assure that one rocking chair is necessarily better than another of similar workmanship and decoration. As we can certainly see in the present, a brand name can mean that a product is "better," but it can also mean that its advertising is superior.

From information contained in account books, store ledgers, and newspaper advertisements, it is clear that rocking chairs were available on a commercial scale by 1820. They were no longer made simply to order, but were produced as a stock item in large business operations. Whether this happened by design of the manufacturers or on demand of the consumer is not known. In an *Albany Register* advertisement of 1815, William Buttre announced that his fancy chair stores in New York and Albany had "constantly for sale, a large assortment of elegant, well-made, and highly finished Black, White, Brown, Coquelico [bright red-orange], Gold, and Eagle Fancy Chairs, Settees, Conversation, Elbow, Rocking, Sewing, Windsor, and Children's Chairs of every description, and on the most reasonable terms."[8]

The Boston Rocker—A New Form

As the rocking chair became more and more popular, its form changed as well. In the eighteenth century, the rocking chair was basically a plain slat-back or Windsor chair with rockers added. But when its production and popularity increased during the early nineteenth century, chairmakers began to look more seriously at its design. Softening the seat and back with a cushion was not the only way to improve its comfort. The seat could be reshaped, the back gently curved to support the lower portion of the spine, and the balance improved. Thus, the Boston rocking chair came into being.

Derived from the Windsor chair, the classic Boston rocker (figure 40) is defined primarily by its rolled seat which curves down at the front and up in the back, to form an S-curve if viewed from the side. It seems that style and need formed a happy combination in this regard, for the shape of the Boston rocker seat is a style-line basic to the Empire period, while the curve helps to support the lumbar portion of the sitter's back. The seat itself, usually of pine, is nearly always one board wide from side to side, but it is made of three pieces of wood from front to back—the curl under and the curve up are separate pieces applied to the main

40. *Left:* "The most popular chair ever made, the type which people use, antiquarians despise, and novices seek," wrote Wallace Nutting of the Boston rocker in his *Furniture Treasury* (Vol. II). When he published these remarks about 1930, he was correct on all four points. Today, however, the Boston rocking chair is not so despised by collectors whose sights go beyond antiques of the seventeenth and eighteenth centuries. He was especially accurate in his first statement: the Boston rocking chair is, indeed, "the most popular chair ever made," for the type survived in proportion, and often in detail, throughout the nineteenth century and even into the twentieth.

41. Rocking chair, probably made in the Connecticut Valley about 1800 and altered later. The desire for stylishness can take many forms. A quick glance at this example might suggest that the rocking chair was made about 1830, when in fact it is an older Windsor armchair modernized by the addition of an Empire-style crest rail and rockers to give the appearance of a Boston rocker.

seat, in part to exaggerate the shape. The roll down in the front is also more comfortable for the underside of the sitter's legs because the front edge of the seat does not force its way into the natural bend behind the knee.

While the comfortable scroll seat is the major defining characteristic of the Boston rocking chair, other elements of the design vary. The Boston rocker usually has either a spindle back, the type most closely akin to its Windsor ancestor, or a single vase-shaped back splat, which makes it look more similar to the Grecian side chairs popular during the period. The design of the Boston rocking chair back, however, is not limited to these two styles. The child's rocking chair in figure 43, for example, shows a clever adaptation of the spindle variety to the Gothic taste with five small pointed arches in the top rail. Although the rocking chair in figure 45 is basically a slat-back type, the extra high back in combination with a slightly rolled rush seat places it on the

fringes of the large Boston-type rocking chair group.

For the most part, early nineteenth-century wooden rocking chairs were painted, as was common in chairs made up of different woods. In contrast to the unornamented paint of eighteenth-century common chairs, nineteenth-century chairs could be quite elaborate. Fancy painted chairs had attained a considerable measure of popularity by 1800, although there are few finely-painted rocking chairs in the Federal style. One defining characteristic of the Empire style is the contrast of light, bright decoration on a dark

42. *The East Parlor of the Peter Cushing House*, painted by Ella Emory in 1878. The Boston rocking chair at the right is outfitted with a long cover overlapping the back with a separate seat cushion to help keep draughts off the sitter during cold winter months. Artifacts made between 1800 and 1870 are arranged in front of a finely paneled fireplace wall of a seventeenth-century house.

background. In expensive high-style furniture this was accomplished through the use of gilt bronze mounts or brass inlay on an ebony, mahogany, or black-enameled surface. The same characteristic contrast was achieved on the common fancy chair through the use of paints and metallic powders (figure 45). Black or rosewood grain-painted grounds were ornamented with gold and bronze metallic powders rubbed with a soft-tipped applicator through stencils cut in a variety of popular motifs—scrolls, flowers, eagles, cornucopias, fruit baskets—which could be used singly or in combination. Striping was often added to highlight the decorative turnings on legs and spindles. The term "Hitchcock chair" is used generically to refer to chairs ornamented in this manner, although Lambert Hitchcock's factory in Hitchcocksville (now Riverton), Connecticut, was only one of the many manufactories of stencil-decorated fancy chairs (figure 46). Since his firm was systematic in labeling its chairs, Hitchcock's name is perhaps more familiar to people today than the maker of any other American chair.

The commercial manufacture of the scroll-seat rocking chair must have begun in Boston during the early 1820s. Although no one maker is credited with development of this new style, its area of popularity and production spread quickly. In many cases, the names given to furniture forms evolved many years after the form itself came into use. The term "Lincoln rocker," for example, has been used only during the last fifty years and was never used in Abraham Lincoln's time. On the other hand, Boston rockers have probably been called that from the time they were first made to denote, if not their point of manufacture, at least their city of birth. "Life at Harvard," wrote Sarah Anna Emery of her experiences there about 1830, "was much more primitive than at present. The dormitories were uncarpeted and furnished with

43. A rolled seat and spindle back identify this unusual Pennsylvania child's rocker with the Boston rocking chair group, while the five small arches in the crest rail are Gothic in execution, a distinctive substyle of the early Victorian period. The extra piece beneath the front of the seat is missing.

44. In the eighteenth century, the infant's caretaker was required to sit separately from the cradle and rock the infant by hand or with her foot. Rocking chair and cradle are combined in this model, probably made in New England about 1840, so that the caretaker can rock in the normal adult rocking motion, while the infant rocks from side to side as it would in a cradle. With the retainer removed, it becomes a rocking settee. The patterns of wear on this well-preserved example indicate that it was used most often in the combined form.

common bedsteads, pine washstands, tables and chairs. What were termed Boston rocking chairs were luxuries recently introduced by some of the students into their rooms."[9]

As soon as the new style appeared in Boston, its popularity began to spread to other areas of the country. In 1830, the merchant Richard Wright of Washington, D.C., advertised "A supply of those much admired high back Boston-made Rocking Chairs which are worthy of the attention of those who love comfort." His advertisement of 1831 leaves no doubt that these "Boston-made" chairs were of the classic Boston style: "JUST received, by the Velocity, from Boston, a handsome lot scroll seat high back Rocking Chairs." That the Boston rocker had migrated westward as well may be seen in John Frewin's report in the *Architec-*

tural Magazine (London) that he had seen them in St. Louis, Missouri, in 1838. "Chairs of this kind," he wrote, "are made chiefly at Boston, which is the great Emporium for furniture in North America."[10]

The popularity of the Boston rocking chair is confirmed by the fact that chairmakers in other parts of the country began to make and advertise the new style. James Canon, a chairmaker of East Caln Township in Chester County, Pennsylvania advertised "large rocking chairs, of the Boston pattern" in 1838. Likewise, Joseph Jones billed Mr. Benjamin Sharpless for "1 Boston Rock Chair bronz [sic] bands $3.75" in West Chester, Pennsylvania. An advertisement for J.C. Gilbert's Utica (New York) Chair Store in the *Utica City Directory* of 1842-43 includes "A variety of

45. The use of bright, classically-inspired decorations on a dark ground is one of the distinguishing characteristics of Empire furniture. On expensive high-style examples this contrast was achieved by the use of gilt bronze mounts, brass inlay, or graceful freehand-painted decoration on mahogany, rosewood, ebony, or painted surfaces. Stenciling with metallic powders on painted black or rosewood grained surfaces produced the same effect on the more common fancy chairs, such as this example of about 1850.

46. Rocking chair labeled "HITCHCOCK • ALFORD & CO
HITCHCOCKS-VILLE • CONN • WARRANTED," 1829-1843.
Windsor-derived rocking chairs of this type with a flat
seat are often called "Salem rockers" to distinguish
them from the similar scroll-seat Boston rockers. The
term "Hitchcock Chair" is used generically by collectors and dealers today to denote painted and stenciled
chairs of the second quarter of the nineteenth century.
However, Lambert Hitchcock's chair manufactory at
Hitchcocksville (now Riverton), Connecticut, was only
responsible for a small proportion of those that were
made in the period and that survive today.

47. Upholstered spring-seat rocking chair with the label of William Hancock, 1829-1833. "Elegance And Ease," ran the headline of an advertisement that appeared in the *Daily National Intelligencer* (Washington, D.C.) of August 20, 1830. "The subscriber has just received direct from the Manufactory, at Boston, a large and handsome assortment of the much admired Spring Seat Rocking Chairs, which combine in a peculiar manner, both Elegance and Ease." This example is indeed a "peculiar" combination of turned rocking chair base, jigsaw-cut scrolled arms, and expensive button upholstery, with very finely stenciled decoration on the front seat rail and at the sides of the rolled crest rail. The high back and scrolled arms of the Boston rocker are present in this chair, but with spring upholstery the characteristic Boston rolled seat was unnecessary.

48. Upholstered rocking chair in which Abraham Lincoln was assassinated, made in America about 1850. The S-curved back, scrolled arms, and suggestive sabre legs are all attributes of the upholstered Grecian-style rocking chair manufactured in the U.S. from about 1830 until 1860. Publication of a photograph of this rocking chair in the early twentieth century led antiquarians to refer to the type as a "Lincoln rocker." Today, the term is wrongly used to denote any Grecian-style rocking chair whether upholstered in lavish fabric or in the more common cane.

Boston Rocking and Nurse Chairs." Many other contemporary advertisements reveal the immense popularity of the Boston rocker in several areas of American by mid-century.[11]

In addition to the Windsor-style Boston rocker, the Washington, D.C., merchant Richard Wright, in 1829, offered "from the celebrated manufactory of William Hancock, of Boston, an assortment of Patent Spring Seat Rocking Chairs, such as have never before been offered in this city, combining comfort and splendor, and of most modern style." William Hancock's spring-seat rocking chairs do indeed "combine in a peculiar manner, both Elegance and Ease." The design of the labeled rocking chair in the Essex Institute (figure 47) incorporates the high back, scrolled arms, and turned legs and stretchers of the "Boston" mode with the elegant upholstery of the more expensive easy chair. An upholstered rocking chair such as the Hancock example substantiates the view that the rocking chair satisfied some of the same needs as the easy chair, though perhaps for a different pocketbook. At the same time, the production of an elegant and expensively upholstered rocking

49. "The Assassination of President Lincoln at Ford's Theatre on the night of April 14, 1865," *Harper's Weekly*, April 29, 1865. "The President sat in the left-hand corner of the box, nearest the audience, in an easy arm-chair," the reporter noted in describing the gruesome murder. The Lincolns had intended to spend a relaxing evening viewing *Our American Cousin* after the surrender of Robert E. Lee to Ulysses S. Grant at Appomattox Court House and the long cabinet meeting at which plans for Southern reconstruction were considered. The rather worn rocking chair had been brought from storage in the manager's office to comfort the tired President.

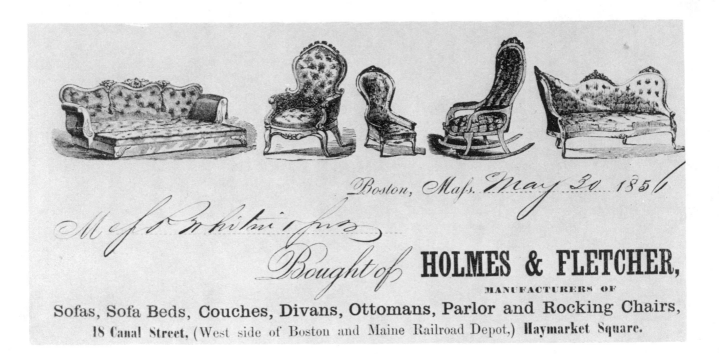

Boston, Mass. *May 30, 1856*

M[s]o Whitn[ ] [ ]s

Bought of **HOLMES & FLETCHER,**

MANUFACTURERS OF

Sofas, Sofa Beds, Couches, Divans, Ottomans, Parlor and Rocking Chairs,

18 Canal Street, (West side of Boston and Maine Railroad Depot,) Haymarket Square.

50. An upholstered Grecian arm rocker is pictured with parlor furniture of a similar class on this billhead, dated 1856, of Holmes & Fletcher, Boston furniture manufacturers.

chair indicates that the form was slowly becoming acceptable as a piece of parlor furniture in high-class urban homes.[12]

Even more elegant in style and workmanship is the upholstered Grecian rocking chair of the kind represented in Edouart's family silhouette, and referred to today as the "Lincoln Rocker" (figure 48). While the Boston rocking chair, including Hancock's "peculiar" version, was derived from the Windsor chair of the eighteenth century, the Grecian variety is essentially a high-contour-back open-arm easy chair with rockers added. These probably appeared in fashionable parlors by 1830. The most expensive examples have front arm supports elaborately carved with swans, double reverse scrolls, eagles, and other neoclassical motifs, while the arms of the more modest versions terminate in bold jig-saw cut scrolls characteristic of the late Empire style (figure 50). The same style could be had in the plainer and less expensive cane seat-and-back variety of the Grecian rocking chair made for country houses, bed chambers, and modest middle-class parlors. The elegant design, combined witht he durable cane seat and back, recommended these simpler versions as a comfortable seat throughout the nineteenth century.

If the eighteenth century was the period in which the fledgling rocking chair seemed to take its first tentative steps, then the early nineteenth century was the period of its charming youth. Decorated and dressed in the latest fashion, the once "ugly duckling" began to assume a new dignity and a real identity. For in the early nineteenth century, chairmakers began to take a hard look at the rocking chair, and what they came up with—the Boston rocker—was a new design which followed the late-Empire fashion and provided greater comfort as a seating form. The seat was designed to blend into the chair back, which was curved to support the human back where it most needed support—in the lumbar region.

Upholstered rocking-chair styles enhanced comfort to a greater degree and obviated the necessity of using loose cushions to mitigate the stiffness of wood. At the same time, upholstery increased the acceptability of the rocking chair in the parlor. As the nineteenth century wore on, more attention was focused on the desire for comfortable seating in formal rooms. The old wooden rocker of the eighteenth century would be nearly unrecognizable by the time that tireless engineers and ambitious upholsterers had finished working their magic.

51. Martha's Vineyard, c. 1880.

3.
What Is Home Without a Rocker?

Two general rocking chair types emerged by the mid-nineteenth century. The standard floor rocker evolved in many varieties from the plain chair with two rockers. The platform, or patent, rocker in which the rocking seat is supported by or suspended above a stationary base, began to be explored as a viable alternative by 1860. Prior to 1850, the standard rocking chair was often a plain chair without upholstery, although there were exceptions, including William Hancock's spring-seat rocking chair and the Grecian-style or so-called "Lincoln" rocker. As the century wore on, however, many types of upholstery were employed to enhance the rocking chair's comfort, and at the same time there appeared several types of upholstered chairs that could have rockers added as an option.

52. That children's furniture often shows more delightfully imaginative design than adult furniture may be seen in this child's rocking chair of the late nineteenth century.

53. Advertisement for Merriam & Parsons, Boston, c. 1875.

Decorative Seats

Woven cane was regularly used on the small woman's rocker by the mid-nineteenth century. Cane is durable, yet decorative as an upholstery material. It is light and clean, resilient, yet relatively inexpensive; so it came well-recommended as a fabric for rocking chairs that were used for prolonged work periods. In *The House Beautiful* (1877), Clarence Cook recommended that "It will be found for good health, and conducive to the freshness and simplicity of a small apartment, to get rid of upholstery and stuffing in our furniture as far as possible." Furniture-trade catalogues leave no question that cane seat-and-back rockers were intended for women. They were variously called "nurse," "sewing," or "slipper" rockers and were generally armless or with diminished arms or brackets well below the level of moving, working elbows. This size and type often appeared in the curved-back Grecian style throughout the second half of the nineteenth

54. George Hunzinger sold this rocker "in maple or walnut, with any color braided wire seat and back," for $8.00. The wire seat offered an alternative to cane as a seating material, but the colored braid which covered the steel strips wore through rather quickly. From J. Wayland Kimball's *Book of Designs: Furniture and Drapery* (Boston, 1876).

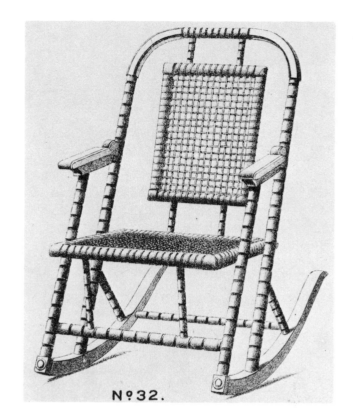

N⁰ 32.

century, but was also well-suited to the more transient fashionable styles of each decade.

Purchased alone or *en suite* in bedroom sets, the common nurse or sewing rocker must have been present in nearly every home by 1870 (figure 13). Many different styles of cane back-and-seat nurse rocking chairs were offered at from $18 to $30 per dozen by Ambrose Barnes of New York, a typical merchant, in his wholesale furniture price list of 1880. Barnes sold Walnut bedroom suites—which included two, three, or four chairs and a rocking chair—for $42.25 to $200, a price range that covered the plainest to the most elaborate styles.

Enameled cottage bedroom suites, advertised by many furniture manufacturers and retailers from about 1850 onward, invariably included a nurse rocker in either all wood or cane back and seat. These sets could be very inexpensive. In 1852, for example, Hart, Ware and Company of Philadelphia offered "complete sets to order [for]

$25 upwards.'' Undoubtedly, many of these enameled or painted bedroom suites were incorporated into middle-class urban apartments, although they were probably fashioned originally for the plainer home in more rural areas. Andrew Jackson Downing in his *Architecture of Country Houses* (1850) called the "fine mahogany chairs and sofas,'' made by city cabinetmakers for townhouses:

the crying sin of all cottage interiors...It is too fine and too town bred for amiable association with country lives and habits. We congratulate the cabinet-makers on the new light which has dawned upon them in the matter of "cottage furniture''—which is now afforded in all our principal cities, of pretty forms and at moderate prices—so that one can furnish a cottage in the country, at short notice, without having it look as if it had been stuffed with chairs and tables sent up from a town house five times its size.[1]

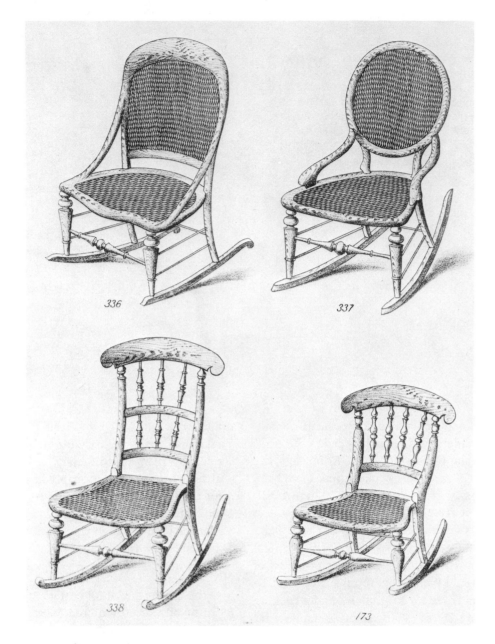

336   337

338   173

55. English rocking chairs were, for the most part, rather plain since they never had the pretensions to elegance shown in their American counterparts. "American rocking chairs," as the English called them, were made in High Wycombe, a well-known chair-making area in England. The examples shown here are from a book of designs bearing the name of James Thomas, "Practical Cabinet maker, Upholsterer, Undertaker, Paperhanger, & c.," and are similar to those illustrated in catalogues of the 1870s issued by Glenister & Gibbons and William Collins & Sons, both High Wycombe firms. Alfred George Edwards, born in 1848, the first Archbishop of Wales, was nursed by his mother in a rocking chair very much like #337.

At least two other materials for the seats and backs of chairs appeared in the later nineteenth century as alternatives to cane. In 1876, George Hunzinger, an eccentric New York chairmaker and designer, patented and introduced a woven steel-band upholstery for chairs and for floor rockers which was intended to provide a more colorful and durable counterpart to woven cane (figure 54). Quarter-inch-wide steel bands covered with a brightly-colored knit fabric were plain woven in a wide-open pattern on seats and sometimes backs of chairs. The new upholstery offered the same openness which recommended cane over stuffed upholstery, and the steel bands were certainly durable as long as they did not come unstrung from their anchor pins. The knitted fabric sleeves, however, were too fragile to survive use over any period of time, so the advantage of color was quickly lost.

Perforated veneer seats were developed by Gardner and Company of Clarksville (now Glen Gardner), New Jersey, to rival woven cane as a clean and durable alternative to fabric upholstery (figure 56). "The seats," proclaimed the company, "do not fade, accumulate dust or get eaten up by moths, as is the case with upholstered-seat chairs." Thin sheets of inexpensive wood were glued and pressed together to make the veneer. Machine drills or punches then perforated the veneer in a variety of primarily geometric patterns, although slogans and names could also be special-ordered. The perforated veneer seats could be quickly tacked onto both seat and back or could be steam bent to make the seat and back a single continuous piece. These processes rendered a product that was made quickly by semi-skilled workmen and was more decorative than cane. Gardner's slogan, "STRONG, ORNAMENTAL, COMFORTABLE AND CLEANLY," summarized the attributes of perforated veneer. The primary image of Gardner and Company's advertising, which showed a small child breaking through a

GARDNER & CO., 183 Canal Street, New York.

No. 224.
No. 225.—Child's.

No. 204.

56. Folding rockers and chairs with perforated veneer seats and backs offered in the 1879 catalogue of Gardner & Company, whose warerooms were in New York City.

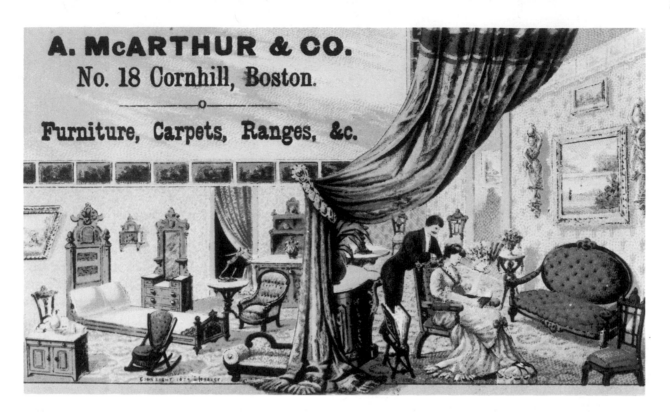

57. "Everybody may have a Nicely Furnished Home"
declares this advertising card for A. McArthur & Company, Boston. An upholstered floor rocker similar to the
model offered by George Hunzinger in the 1870s is pictured in the bedroom setting at the left.

cane seat while reaching for the proverbial cookie jar, was probably meaningful to many mothers. Unfortunately, veneer had its drawbacks as well. It warped, cracked, and splintered so that it became a hazard for skin as well as for clothing and presented a dilapidated appearance. In the end its real advantages were that it could be made more ornamental than cane and that it could be used as a homemaker-installed replacement for worn-out cane.

Elaborately-upholstered floor rockers also began to appear in the parlor with more regularity after 1850. Generally, these were easy chairs with arms and an inclined back, although a few man-ufacturers, such as George Hunzinger of New York, offered stylish armless rocking chairs upholstered, buttoned, and fringed in the latest fashion to be used as side chairs in the parlor (figure 60). In their 1878 catalogue, the Phoenix Furniture Company of Grand Rapids, Michigan, advertised the curved rococo and angular Renaissance Revival styles among their upholstered armless rockers. The "Lincoln" or Grecian-style rocking armchair continued to be made in some fashion through the 1860s, while other upholstered types, such as the "Spanish" or "Sleepy Hollow" rockers achieved fame for briefer periods of time in the 1860s and 1870s (figure 61).[2]

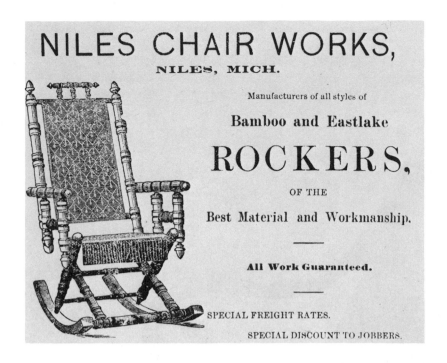

NILES CHAIR WORKS,
NILES, MICH.

Manufacturers of all styles of

Bamboo and Eastlake
ROCKERS,
OF THE

Best Material and Workmanship.

———

All Work Guaranteed.

———

SPECIAL FREIGHT RATES.

SPECIAL DISCOUNT TO JOBBERS.

58. *Above:* The influence of Charles L. Eastlake's *Hints on Household Taste*, first published in 1868 in London, was so pervasive in America that his name was used indiscriminately by furniture purveyors to suggest simple suitability and handsome craftsmanship. Eastlake, however, would probably not have approved of the "Eastlake" chair advertised by the Niles Chair Works in the *Michigan Artisan* for June, 1884.

59. *Right:* Woodcut from a small brochure for the Philadelphia merchants Sanderlin & Van Loan, about 1870.

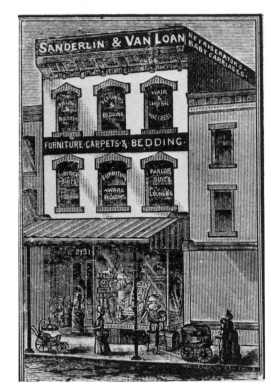

60. George Hunzinger of New York offered this upholstered floor rocker in J. Wayland Kimball's *Book of Designs: Furniture and Drapery* (1876). The frame could be purchased in walnut for $13.33, with upholstery "in Muslin, $24.00; in Terry, with nice bordering, $33.33."

61. Washington Irving once owned this mid-nine-teenth-century contour rocking chair fixed in a reclined position. Because of this, the type later became known as a "Sleepy Hollow" rocker.

62. *Right:* Upholstered rocking chairs of the mid-nineteenth century were often conceived, like their eighteenth-century counterparts, as chairs with rockers added. This example is typical of upholstered rocking side chairs in the Rococo-Revival style appropriate for a parlor.

SPANISH ROCKERS.
From $10 upwards,

63. In its own day the so-called "Sleepy Hollow" rocker was actually referred to as a "Spanish Rocker." From a catalogue and almanac for 1874 of John F. Mason & Company, Brooklyn, New York.

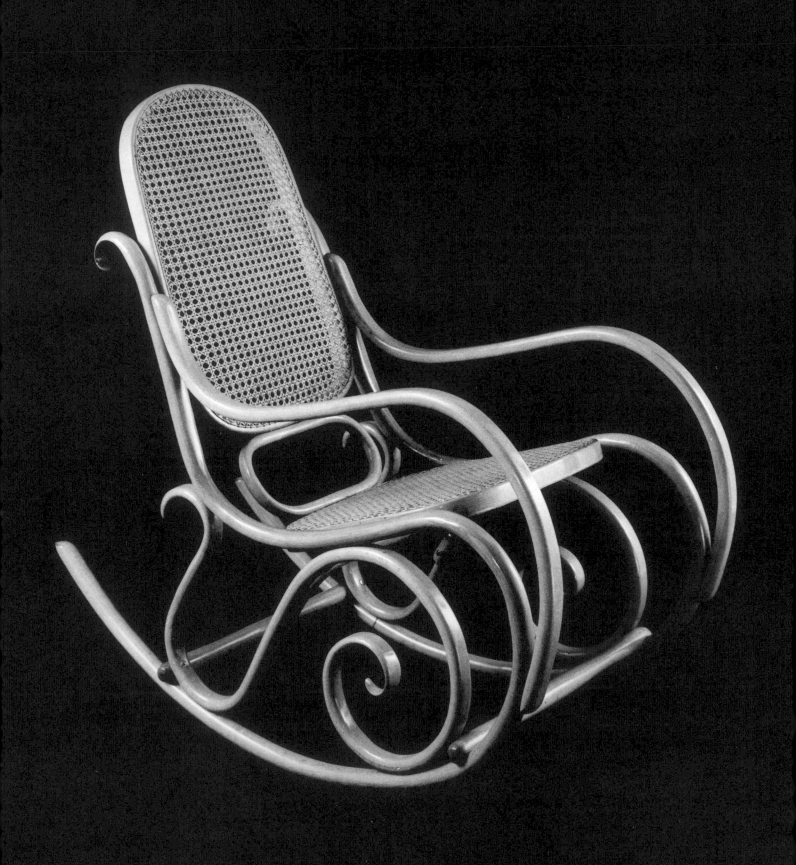

64. *Opposite:* Michael Thonet's innovative rocking-chair design of 1859 has had lasting appeal for consumers. He was the first designer to consider the decorative potential of the rockers.

65. Child's bentwood rocking chair with the label of Thonet Brothers. Constituent parts of this rocker were made in Vienna and shipped to New York for assembly in the late nineteenth century. The paper label states, "Thonet, Wien. 860 Broadway, cor 17th Street, N.Y./ Beware of imitations. No goods genuine without trade mark/ which assures highest standard of workmanship and quality./ Salesroom for the United States and Canada." Although Thonet perfected the process of steam-bending beechwood, it was employed by other European and American chair manufacturers, such as Jacob and Joseph Kohn of Vienna, Thonet's biggest competitor in the late nineteenth century.

Bentwood Rockers

The bentwood rocking chair, designed and first marketed by Michael Thonet, is one of the most successful rocking chairs ever developed. In 1836, in a small village on the Rhine, this young cabinetmaker invented the process of making molded-plywood furniture out of wood-veneer strips saturated with warm glue and shaped and cooled in wooden molds. Furniture parts thus made were assembled into chairs that were durable, light, and inexpensive. In 1841, Thonet's process and designs became known to Austrian Chancellor Clemens Metternich who induced him to move to Vienna to work on the restoration of the Liechtenstein Palace. Between 1842 and 1847, Thonet applied his knowledge of mold-shaping laminated woods to the production of solid-wood furniture of steamed European beechwood. The fame of his furniture-making process became world-wide as a result of his display at the Great Exhibition at London's Crystal Palace in 1851.

During the next few decades Thonet and his sons, as the firm of Gebrüder Thonet, expanded their operation over central Europe. Their New York showroom opened in 1853.[3]

The now classic Thonet bentwood rocking chair (figure 64) has been in nearly continuous production since its introduction in 1860. Though small at first, consumer demand grew steadily until, in the 1890s, the estimated annual production was 20,000 rocking chairs. World War II, which interrupted industrial manufacturing all over Europe, was the only period when these famous chairs were not made. This enduring rocking chair design raises questions about the difference between the survival and revival of furniture styles. Although there has in recent years been a renewed interest in bentwood rocking chairs, the modern Thonet product could hardly be considered a revival since it has been produced continuously for over a hundred years.

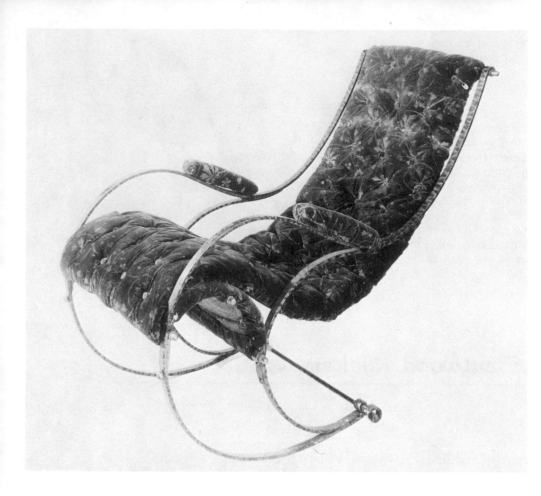

66. Bent-iron rocking chairs, which were shown in 1851 at the Crystal Palace Exhibition in London, are thought to be the inspiration for Thonet's famous bent-beechwood design. R. W. Winfield and Company of Birmingham, England, and William Cunning of Edinburgh offered them in 1851. In America, Herman Berg and Richard Hoffman were issued patents for very similar chairs in 1867. They emphasized that the rocker could be disassembled for transport and that the sling seat was adjustable.

The sensuous and exciting multiple curves of Thonet's design appealed to European and American consumers through a variety of seemingly radical style changes because this rocking chair is so exceedingly comfortable. It is at once a rocker and a recliner, without the mechanical gadgetry which characterized most other types that claimed similar satisfaction. Available in cane, fabric, or leather upholstery, the Thonet rocker continues to complement most interiors.

Furniture historians credit Thonet's inspiration to the bent-metal rocking chair developed in Europe in the 1840s (figure 66). Examples of this bent-metal type were shown in London at the Great Exhibition by R. W. Winfield and Company, of Birmingham, England, and William Cunning, of Edinburgh. In the *Official Catalogue* of the Exhibition, Cunning's chair was described as an "Improved iron rocking-chair, for the drawing-room, in gold, covered with French brocatel. In this chair the spine and back are supported, and the head and neck rest in a natural position." It was designated, as one might expect, "as a useful invention for invalids and others" because Englishmen did not consider that the rocking chair was a suitable seat for healthy adults. At least one example of this chair has a small metal label identifying it as "Dr. Calvert's Digestive Chair." The identity of Dr. Calvert is uncertain since he did not patent his design, but the idea of rocking as an aid to digestion is provocative at least and imaginative at best.[4]

In 1867, Herman Berg, of Springfield, Massachusetts, and Richard Hoffman, of New York, were issued patents for a chair of similar design. "This invention," wrote Berg and Hoffman, "consists in a rocking-chair the frame of which is composed of two side-pieces which are made of thin and elastic strips of metal or wood, and united together by cross-bars which can be readily removed, if desired, in such a manner that a chair is obtained which is very comfortable and easy to sit in, and which can be easily packed up in a comparatively small compass for transportation." The seat and back were formed of one "piece of stout cloth, canvas, leather, or other suitable flexible material." In addition to its transportability, the chair was distinguished by its adjustable seat. "The flexible back can also be readily adjusted by unfastening one of its ends, and giving to it more or less slack, or one end may be secured to a rod which may be so adjusted that by turning the same the back receives more or less slack, and by these means said back can be easily brought in such a position that the centre of gravity of the person sitting in the chair is thrown in the proper relation towards the runners, a point which is of the greatest importance in a good rocking-chair, for if the centre of gravity is too far in the rear, the chair is liable to tip over behind, or at least to assume an uncomfortable position." This rocking chair design was used in America and Europe. Peter Cooper, the New York manufacturer, inventor, and philanthropist, had one, now preserved at the Cooper-Union which he founded. The Andersen Museum in Odense, Denmark, owns one used by Hans Christian Andersen, with the kind of loose fabric seat described by Berg and Hoffman.[5]

Patent Rocking Chairs

Few furniture forms have fired the imagination of American inventors to the extent that the rocking chair did in the nineteenth century. Between 1831 and 1905, more than three-hundred patents were issued for rocking chairs or attachments that made use of the rocking motion. These new chairs not only rocked—they rolled, reclined, swiveled, played music, circulated air, assumed a variety of positions, and converted to cradles, trunks, library steps, beds, and couches. Although the interest in adapting this form spans more than sixty-five years of Patent Office records, two-thirds of the patents were issued in the 1870s and 1880s—during the most competitive period of rocking-chair manufacture.

In his discussion of nineteenth-century patent furniture in *Mechanization Takes Command*, Siegfried Giedion draws an oversimplified distinction between what he calls the monumental "transitory" furniture of the ruling classes and the inventive "constituent" furniture of the middle-class engineer:

The unexplored complex of patent furniture stands apart from the ruling taste. It called forth nearly all the constituent powers of the century. It revealed the century as it liked to relax when wearing none of its masks. This patent furniture tackled problems in a manner completely new to the century.... Furniture was dissected into separate elements, into separate planes. These movable elements, which a governing mechanism linked and regulated, enabled the furniture to change in adaptation to the body and various postures. The furniture was thus endowed with a flexibility unknown before, and ceased to be a rigid, static implement...it could take on any desired position of the human body, change from this position and return to the normal. Comfort actively wrested by adaptation to the body, as against comfort passively derived from sinking back into cushions—here is the whole difference between the constituent furniture and the transitory furniture of the last century.[6]

Motion, adaptability, and mechanization are the distinguishing characteristics of late nineteenth-century rocking chairs as well, for the revolution of which Giedion writes is the revolution in seating furniture, and it began in the early and continuing developments in rocking chair design.

Invalid Rockers

While early nineteenth-century rocking chairs were being stenciled, upholstered, and otherwise varied according to decorative fashion, things began to happen underneath as well. For over a hundred years the basic rocker concept had been adhered to—straight chair with rockers added. Then, with the Boston rocking chair, efforts were made to enhance the form as a more comfortable seat; the rockers remained virtually the same, except for some variation in length to solve problems of stability. But what of "the lower part of this engine," as Daniel Harrington called it?

Harrington, a Philadelphian, was perhaps the first nineteenth-century inventor to focus his attention on the base of the rocking chair. Instead of using conventional legs, Harrington's invention, patented in 1831, consisted of "three pair of elliptical springs made of steel [which]...forms,

together with the rocker beneath, a spring leg, and both of them a pair of spring legs...calculated to give a rolling or rocking motion or perpendicular motion according the the exertion of the invalid occupying the seat above." He called his "machine" a "health vehicle," whereby "invalids in their rooms, houses, or yards of their houses...may derive the healthful (life-giving) exercise (principle) that is usually received from riding upon the back of a trotting or rocking horse, or in a two or four wheeled carriage." Because of the spring legs, the health vehicle served two purposes, first as a conventional rocking chair, and second as an exercise chair on which the invalid could bounce up and down. Exercise chairs "for giving motion or exercise to invalids in their rooms of confinement" developed in the eighteenth century, but they were stationary in the sense that they only moved up and down. Harrington's invention, a combination of wagon springs, saddle, and rockers, was the first of many convertible invalid rocking chairs to appear in the patent records of the nineteenth century.[7]

That the rocking chair continued to have some association with invalids through the years may be seen in Charles Grawitz's recommendation concerning his rocking chair patent of 1870: "it will also be admirably adapted to the use of a sick-room, as it rocks easier, and allows the person sitting in the same to lean back farther, and gives more satisfaction and comfort than the common rocking or easy chair." In 1873 Abel Russell showed similar concern in the letters patent for his folding rocking chair: "The nature of my invention consists in so constructing a folding rocking-chair as to be susceptible of being adjusted to any desired angle to suit the comfort of the invalid, and also the easy manner with which it can be converted into the most perfect and comfortable rocking-couch without the necessity of the invalid being removed." These instances,

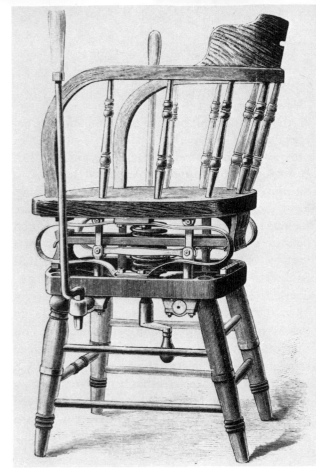

67. A "Health Jolting Chair," advertised in the illustrated catalogue of George F. Sanders, New York, about 1890, was considered a "P_{ERFECT} means of giving E_{FFI-}CIENT exercise to the E_{SSENTIALLY} N_{UTRITIVE} O_{RGANS} O_F T_{HE} B_{ODY.}" Daniel Harrington's spring leg rocking chair of 1831 was intended to provide the same benefits.

however, refer to rocking chairs made primarily for vigorous adults that could serve double-duty as invalid chairs. There was a separate class of rocking chair, however, made exclusively for disabled persons.[8]

A number of rocking-chair patents issued during the late nineteenth century were referred to specifically as "invalid chairs." While some were quite elaborate, all included the ability to support a reclining posture. In 1856, Martin Eberhard of Philadelphia patented an "Improved Chair for Rocking and Reclining" for invalids. It included an "adjustable foot rest, which can be raised and lowered to any desirable position by the foot, and which is combined with the chair in such a way, that the weight of the occupant will retain it in any given position..., a new mode of keeping the chair in a rocking motion by a slight action of the heel, without other exertion to the body and without bringing the foot to the ground, and...a new mode of giving the chair a reclined position by means of a small crank, which is in convenient reach for the occupant of the chair."[9]

T. W. Currier's invalid chair of 1858 could rock, roll around on casters, or be completely stationary as it allowed the occupant to recline in four different positions, including recumbent. "An ordinary rocking and invalid chair," according to A. S. Smith's description of his idea patented the same year, could be made "capable of being converted by a simple adjustment of parts, into a cradle." As in the eighteenth century, convertibility in furniture was a trait consumers admired as much for its ingenious engineering as for the time and space it was intended to save. Although these invalid chairs could be thoughtful and intricate, they were only a small part of the whole phenomenon of patented rocking chairs. The platform rocker, as we shall see, received a good deal more attention from furniture engineers than did these various reclining rockers.[10]

Platform Rockers

As the rocking chair became more and more an acceptable piece of parlor furniture, a number of problems with its size and design became painfully obvious to consumers. Inventors were quick to alleviate these problems by developing the platform rocker, "that class of chairs in which the rockers rest on a base or supporting frame," which became a popular addition to many parlors for a variety of reasons (figure 69). Philadelphian Samuel H. Bean, one of the earliest inventors to devise the platform rocker, noted in his patent of 1840 that his stationary base rocker would do "away with the long and cumbersome rockers on the common chair, which occupy a great deal of room and are very destructive to carpets." In 1858 I. P. Carrier summarized other benefits of this new breed of rocking chair: "The advantage derived from this improvement, over others now in use are: It has no rockers over which persons are liable

68. A rocking chair on concealed springs of the same type offered by Charles White, of Philadelphia, in his *Upholstery and Furniture Bazaar* price list of 1854.

69. Upholstered platform rocking chair suitable for the parlor, American, c. 1880.

to stumble and fall, and under which children not infrequently get their fingers hurt. Also it is not liable to get broken as those with rockers. It has also the advantage of the stationary chair and may be provided with casters to correspond with other furniture."[11]

The new platform idea began to develop momentum after 1850. Not only did it eliminate carpet-damaging rockers, it could, more importantly, be made inconspicuous in a parlor setting. In fact the earliest platform rockers, as well as the more successful later models, were virtually indistinguishable from other upholstered parlor furniture. Charles H. White of Philadelphia offered

"Rocking Chairs on concealed springs" for $45 in his *Upholstery and Furniture Bazaar* price list of 1854. These were expensively upholstered on rosewood, walnut, or mahogany frames. The chair portion rocked upon a stationary base. Fabric to match the upholstery was loosely stretched between the bottom of the chair and the top of the base so that when the chair was unoccupied it looked like a regular Rococo Revival easy chair with very short legs and a large bottom section. Very few survive, perhaps because this design was not the ideal solution to the problem of covering up the chair's real purpose from the discerning eye. Too vigorous motion in rocking backwards

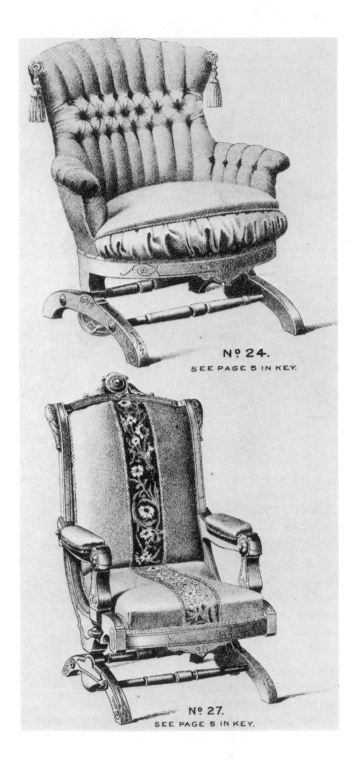

N⁰ 24.
SEE PAGE 5 IN KEY.

N⁰ 27.
SEE PAGE 5 IN KEY.

70. *Left:* When J. Wayland Kimball compiled his *Book of Designs: Furniture and Drapery* in 1876, he noted that "Foreigners call the rocking chair a peculiarly American luxury, yet the necessary length of the rockers on the floor causes this favorite chair to be occasionally in the way, and not infrequently too noisy for comfort. These disadvantages have been ingeniously overcome in the chairs of certain makers, who, in different ways, build them so that there is no rocker on the floor and the movements are always noiseless." He mentioned three firms especially — M. & H. Schrenkeisen, Frank Rhoner and Company, and Palmer and Embury. The two rockers shown here were available from Frank Rhoner and Company of New York.

71. Platform rockers were frequently made with cane seats and backs, as in this plain example illustrated in the 1887 catalogue of G. Stomps and Company, a Dayton, Ohio, firm.

must have ripped a number of the base covers to the consternation and embarrassment of the Victorian hostess (figure 68).

While White's furniture was generally very expensive, the rocking chair on concealed springs at $45 was in the middle range for seating forms in his catalogue. For the most part, platform rockers were not cheap, primarily because of the upholstery. For example, Frank Rhoner and Company's Patent Rocker No. 2, included in *Kimball's Book of Designs* (1876), listed the price of the frame at $10, whereas the plainest upholstery fabric pushed the cost to $26, with the top price for "Plush or Coteline" quoted at $42 (figure 70). The choice of "Terry, with Stripe" upholstery added an additional $10.34 cost to the basic $9.33 frame of M. & H. Schrenkeisen's "Medium Sized Patent Rocker."

No doubt it was such high prices as these—the country was still recovering from the devastating Panic of 1873—that sent Mrs. C. S. Jones into a fury over patent rockers in her *Beautiful Homes, or Hints in House Furnishing* (1878):

For the mother's sitting-room chair, what can ever take the place of the old "rocker"? Yet there certainly will be another beatitude added to the list, by the notable housekeepers, when some ingenious woman (why not a woman?) invents a rocker that will entirely supersede the forked, horned and spiked affair which has occupied space and ruined walls, furniture and feet for the past centuries. We know full well that there have been several patents taken out for chairs, the rockers of which are invisible, or, at least, so constructed that they do not rest upon the floor nor project into interminable space before and behind the seat; but this is not the article required unless indeed such chairs can be made at so low a price that they may be procured quite as cheaply as the rocker now in common use.

These patent rocking-chairs are far too expensive to be purchased by the "million" who most require them, consequently they are never seen save in the houses of the wealthy; and those who procure their pieces of furniture "by the hardest", go on from day to day, having veneering broken out, holes ground into polished panels and the walls worn into chasms, with the incessant vibrations of those great horns in the rear, for *rock* women will, especially if there is a baby in the question. We would say, though, to every woman who can possibly raise the amount of money required for it, to purchase one of the patent rocking-chairs (for her sitting-room at least), for she will find it money *well spent*.

Every part of the base and rocking mechanism of the platform rocker came under the scrutiny of the mechanical engineer during the second half of the nineteenth century. The object of this investigation was to produce a platform rocker "which shall be neat and simple in construction, and safe and reliable in use." To this end inventors employed a variety of springs—described as spiral, coil, elliptical, zigzag, serpentine—which operated either vertically or horizontally. Platform-rocker inventions fall into two general classes. First are those which are actually upholstered seats in rocking frames connected by springs and usually movable parts to a stationary base. The second class consists of those which are flat-bottomed upholstered chairs raised above and connected to a stationary base by a series of strong continuous steel bands coiled or sprung in various ways. Few of these patented rocking devices ever achieved much prominence; and, in fact, inventors were rarely able to sell their ideas to manufacturers. Many devices were clearly unworkable, while others were too complicated to permit profitable production. Often those inventors who succeeded were able to capitalize on very simple solutions.

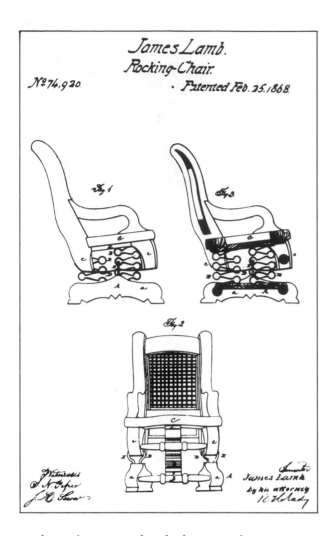

72. Zigzag springs support the chair above its platform and provide a rocking motion, although, as the patentee suggests, "the chair is not confined to a tilting motion in one plane only, but, by my arrangement and combination of springs, may be tilted in various directions. Furthermore, the zigzag springs are peculiarly favorable for the vibratory movements of the chair-seat, and are very much better than helical or spiral springs for such use." James Lamb of Hubbardstown, Massachusetts, received patent #74,920 for this device on February 25, 1868.

As an inventor of a platform mechanism, W.I. Bunker is a conspicuous exception to the norm. Bunker, through J. Beiersdorf, a Chicago furniture manufacturer, advertised "the celebrated B. & B. PATENT ROCKER SPRING" throughout the 1880s. Bunker and Beiersdorf incorporated the device in their platform-rocker design and marketed the device separately to other furniture manufacturers through The Rocker Spring Company, an adjunct to Beiersdorf's furniture business. The B. & B. Patent Rocker Spring was an alarmingly simple coiled spring which attached at its top to the rocking frame and and at its bottom to the platform base at the pivot point between the two pieces of the platform rocker. "The springs measure 2½ inches in diameter," declared the advertisement, "and are made of the best *Oil Tempered Steel*, are practically *one piece, easily put on any Platform Rocker*, and will not *'sing'* or *squeak*, being perfectly *mute*; they are so *simple* that they *can not get out of order* and are nearly *indestructible*. While holding the *Rocker firmly to the Platform* they are no impediment to a *long free swing*, and need no *'Guides,' 'Rubbers,' 'Balances,' 'Weights'* or other *Contrivances* to give satisfaction....The leading Eastern and Western Manufacturers use them. They are a success. Try them. Sold at 50 Cents a Pair." In 1883, B. & B.

73. George Hunzinger patented and produced a number of devices in the late nineteenth century. The paper labels on his duplex spring stationary base rockers recommended that "One drop oil from your Sewing Machine can in every joint of hinge will prevent noise."

claimed 350,000 in use. Many platform rockers which survive are fitted with these uncomplicated springs. All, however, may not be of B. & B. manufacture since the device is so simple that there were undoubtedly patent infringements. Double springs, "Designed for Turkish Rockers," were available for 75¢ each.[12]

Theodore J. Palmer's "oscillating chair" (figure 75) was an unusual device among platform rockers for it did not employ springs between the rocking chair and the base in what came to be the conventional manner. Compared with others, Palmer's device was ingeniously simple. "This invention," he wrote in 1870, "consists in providing for the rocking or adjustment of the inclination of the back and seat of a chair relatively to the base to which they are pivoted by means of arms composed of springs." The base and seat sections were connected by a simple pivot where they met, while the elastic spring-steel arms were connected

85

74. *Above:* The gentleman on the left of this chromolithograph is playing cards while seated in one of Palmer's patent spring-arm rocking chairs. The card player on the right rises from a wicker rocker.

75. "Palmer's Patent Rocker and Reclining Chair No. 2, is here represented as upholstered with a fine broche stripe inserted in Terry and puffed sides, spring seat and back, price $29.33; same in Plush with Satin stuffing, $38.67." So read the caption for this illustration in Kimball's *Book of Designs* (1876).

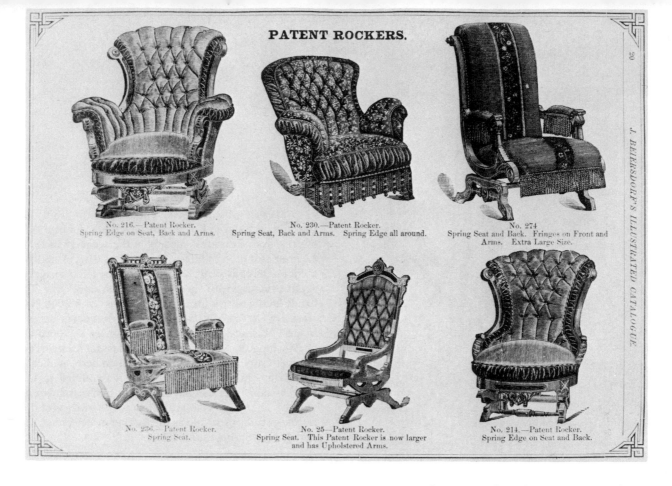

No. 216.—Patent Rocker.
Spring Edge on Seat, Back and Arms.

No. 230.—Patent Rocker.
Spring Seat, Back and Arms. Spring Edge all around.

No. 274
Spring Seat and Back. Fringes on Front and Arms. Extra Large Size.

No. 236.—Patent Rocker.
Spring Seat.

No. 25—Patent Rocker.
Spring Seat. This Patent Rocker is now larger and has Upholstered Arms.

No. 214.—Patent Rocker.
Spring Edge on Seat and Back.

76. A group of patent rockers from J. Beiersdorf's *Illustrated Catalogue* of 1882. These models undoubtedly included the Bunker & Beiersdorf patented rocker spring.

to the front of the base frame at their lower ends and mid-way up the back of the chair section at their upper ends. When the chair section was moved backward or forward on its pivot "a tension [was] produced on the spring arms, which tend[ed] to replace the back and seat to their former position, thus facilitating the easy rocking of the chair to the person sitting therein." Although the back of the chair section did not operate separately from the seat, the sitter could, by the use of clamps, fix the chair section in a reclined position. The whole spring arms of

Palmer's patent rocker were covered with fabric and the arm-rests could be "cushioned, as the arms of rocking-chairs usually are." Palmer's invention was one of the few successful patent rocker designs which actually went into production. It was offered in the 1870s by the firm of Palmer and Embury of New York. Frames could be purchased for $13.33 or upholstered in several ways, ranging in price from $26.66 to $38.67.[13]

Patent rockers of the 1870s were usually sold as separate pieces of furniture so that they could be suitably placed in several rooms of the house. In

87

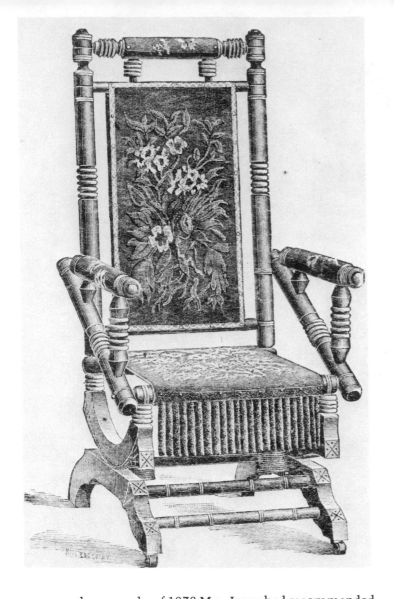

77. "Success was never ripe enough to drop from the tree" was the slogan B.A. Atkinson adopted for himself. His rise from a mattress repairer at the age of 18 in 1873 to proprietor of "the largest house furnishing establishment on the continent, having a combined floor space of about 10 acres with 3 spacious elevators, employing 300 hands and facilities for doing a business of $2,000,000 annually" in 1887, is one of the great American success stories. Atkinson's factory and warehouses were located on Washington Street in Boston, Massachusetts. The "Velvet Carpet" platform rocker shown here, available in "ebony, mahogany or walnut" was offered to his middle-class American buying public in his catalogue of c. 1882. The spring visible just below the fringe is of the uncomplicated type sold as the Bunker & Beiersdorf Patent Rocker Spring in the 1880s.

her remarks of 1878 Mrs. Jones had recommended them for use in a "sitting-room at least," suggesting that for those who considered the rocking chair unsuitable for the parlor, concessions could be made in the more personal rooms of a house. For those families who were conscious of the traditional bias against the use of rockers in formal rooms, patent rocking chairs were elegantly upholstered. Giedion's polar distinctions between "transitory" and "constituent' furniture in the nineteenth century collapse in a consideration of the patent rocker, which combined the "comfort passively derived from sinking back into cushions" with the "comfort actively wrested by adaptation to the body."

As growing numbers of consumers considered the rocking chair an essential furniture form for the parlor, manufacturers began to market parlor suites which could include matching patent rockers (figure 78). There were a number of companies such as Butler Brothers of Chicago (1891-2) that offered suites including a "large double back sofa, divan, rocker, easy chair, and parlor chair [in] oak, XVI century or mahogany finish." Each piece

78. The *Specialties in Furniture* catalogue issued in 1891 by Butler Brothers of Chicago carried this illustration of the "Mansion Parlor Suit," which could be purchased for $152.

was "luxuriously upholstered in Wilton rug." Those buyers with more space could add a second and third parlor chair to enlarge the suite to seven pieces. Parlor suites with rockers to match appeared on the market in the 1870s, but became less expensive and thus more popular during the 1880s and 1890s. Modern furniture companies to this day, in fact, continue to offer living room suites which can include rockers.[14]

Rockers for Convenience

Folding rocking chairs form another subgroup within the patented rocking chair inventions that proliferated in the 1870s and '80s. As a compact and readily expandable seating form, folding chairs offer the consumer many advantages. They can be conveniently stored and easily transported to be used elsewhere or even out of doors. While light in weight, they can also be sturdy in construction. Inventors concentrated on finding ways to make the chair compact and uncomplicated. "The construction of the chair is exceedingly simple," wrote David Selleg of his patent model in 1878. "There are no extra parts to get out of order, and the chair can be made very strong and substantial."[15]

In the year 1881 alone, at least seven patents were issued for rocking chairs which folded in a variety of ways. Some had cross-legs, some had straight chair legs with cross braces to the back, some had rigid seats, some had flexible or slack seats. All had movable joints that slid through slots or pivoted on pins. One added attraction was the manner in which these folding chairs could be enhanced with arms. Clifford C. Nichols of Cincinnati, Ohio, promised that his folding rocking chair "combines, with an ordinary back and pair of rockers, a uniting brace piece of ogee form, so as to constitute a triangular rigid truss on each side of the chair, and in which said ogee brace-pieces are further serviceable as chair-arms." According to the patent drawing of 1878, Nichols' folding rocking chair—designed in the Grecian manner with front sabre legs—could fold in a long, flat space. The folding rocker patented in 1876 by Nicholas, Claudius, and Adam Collignon (figure 81) had the familiar Grecian shape, but the front sabre legs were formed by the broadly-curving arms attached near the rockers to cross braces. The Collignons, who maintained a thriving folding-chair business in Closter, New Jersey, were concerned that "A rocking-chair with arms, as ordinarily constructed, is cumbersome and unwieldy to move

79. Child's folding rocker with cane seat and back. The underside of the seat frame is branded "COLLIGNON's. PATENT/ MAR. 10.68 & Nov. 16.69" (See figure 81.)

80. *Above:* Collignon Brothers' Manufactories at Closter, New Jersey, from C. C. Pease's *Atlas of Bergen County, New Jersey* (1876). Collignon Brothers specialized in the manufacture of folding chairs, which were produced in New Jersey and sold through their warerooms in New York City.

81. Nicholas, Claudius, and Adam Collignon's folding rocking-chair patent #176,929, dated May 2, 1876, shows the manner in which the arms were made as part of the design.

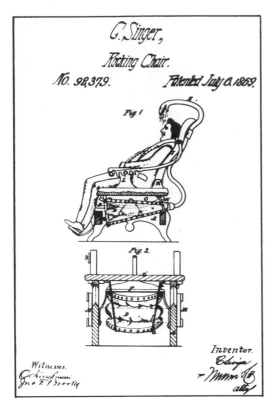

G. Singer,
Rocking Chair.
No. 92,379.   Patented July 6, 1869.

Fig 1

Fig 2

Witnesses.

Inventor.

82. What could be more refreshing than to have a stream of circulating air blow over you as you rock? This pleasing thought prompted a number of inventors to analyze the problem and devise some rather comical solutions. The device illustrated was patented by Charles Singer of South Bend, Indiana, July 6, 1869.

from place to place...." "When shipped," they observed, rocking chairs "occupy much valuable space that might otherwise be saved. To obviate these disadvantages we construct our arm rocking-chair so that it may be folded into a compact shape, occupying comparatively little space, and admitting of its easy transportation."[16]

Air-Circulating Rockers

Because it moved, the rocking chair also provided a vehicle for circulating air. No less than twenty-three patents were issued between 1847 and 1906 to enable the rocking chair's occupant to swirl and refresh the air around him. When Charles Horst, a New Orleans resident, patented his complicated apparatus in 1847, he claimed that the mechanism would throw a "puff of air to the rear into the face of the person seated in the chair, imparting a refreshing coolness, and at the same time

dispelling those horrible pests of the south, mosquitoes...thus the operation of rendering one's self comfortable in a hot and sultry climate is continued by the pleasant recreation of rocking one's self in a chair." Before the days of climate-controlled and insulated environments, "flies and insects in the air [were] an annoyance to a person while sitting in a chair," whether in Louisiana or in New York. In 1869 Martin Steifenhofer of the latter city noted in his patent application that irritation from insects was "frequently the case when sitting in a rocking-chair, the motion thereof being insufficient to drive away such insects."[17]

Many patented air-circulating devices employed the motion of regular floor rockers with the fan mechanism attached to the arm, back, or sides of the chair. These ranged from the simplicity of Mary Ann Woodward's "Aeolian" of 1849, a weighted curtain suspended on a frame rising from the back of the rocking chair, to the useless com-

83. Each of the businessmen in the foreground of this c. 1910 photograph is seated in a rocking chair. The rocker on the left is obvious, while the one on the right is disguised as a stationary-base chair. Chair seat and arms are the same on both.

plexity of David Kahnweiler's "Magic Ventilator" of 1857. In Kahnweiler's incredible olfactory device, a bellows attached between the rockers forced air through a tube running beneath the rocking chair and thence upward into a box-like chamber mounted on a stand in front of it. A nozzle aimed at the chair's occupant was the final fixture in the process of "conveying atmospheric air through a body of ice or other cooling materials [in the chamber], coming in contact with some etheric substance or other choice perfume, impregnating the same with grateful odor rendering it salutary and refreshing."[18]

Bellows were also included in platform rocking chairs because they could be more easily hidden within the chair's base frame. Charles Singer's 1869 contrivance circulated air from the bellows through a pipe behind and over the top of the chair (figure 82). Although the occupant of this chair in the patent illustration seems to be enjoying the cooling effects of the snake's breath above him, suggesting that the purpose of the apparatus was pleasure pure and simple, Singer claimed that the importance of his machine lay in the "arrangement whereby the parts may be readily detached for storage or packing in compact form."[19]

84. ''Revolving, Rocking and Tilting'' chair offered by the Detroit Chair Factory, Detroit, Michigan, about 1880. The chair was advertised as being ''particularly adapted to the court room, lodge room, office, library, dining room, in fact to any position when ease and comfort [was] a desideratum.''

Clayton Denn of Frankford, Pennsylvania, invented an improved rocking chair in 1870 constructed so that ''its motion [might] be utilized for working a bellows and producing music.'' In addition to the automatic operation of the bellows, Denn's invention was supplied with ''keys on the sides of the chair, and of stops for throwing the bellows out of gear or into action.'' Consumers of his musical device, if indeed there were any, might have been more pleased to know that there was a lever to ''arrest the motion of the bellows'' and hence to shut off the pneumatic serenade. [20]

Office Rockers

During the nineteenth century, the rocking chair continued to be adapted to various needs and situations, and the gentleman's office was no exception (figure 83). Peter Ten Eyck was one of the first inventors to devise a mechanism whereby a low-back Windsor, or captain's, chair was supported on a pedestal ''so arranged as that the top or seat shall rock upon the bottom part while the legs remain stationary.'' In addition, Ten Eyck's invention of 1853 provided ''a safety guard, to prevent the chair from going suddenly backward when the person seats himself in it.'' A vertical screw rod allowed the chair seat to be raised and lowered in much the same fashion as those in use today. Several other oscillating office-chair inventions, such as the one patented by P. G. Ingersoll of Greenpoint, New York in 1872, rotated as well as rocked. The seat of another, produced by the Shakers of Mt. Lebanon, New York, could rotate, raise, and lower; however, it rocked by the addition of rockers to the legs rather than by a device connected to the seat. [21]

Patented convertible furniture could perform combinations of many functions by the 1880s. One of the most elaborate examples of this phenomenon was the ''Rip Van Winkle Reclining Rocking Chair,'' ''THE CHAIR FOR EVERYBODY, being ELEGANT, COMPLETE AND CHEAP'' (figure 87). Patented in 1887 and 1888 and manufactured by P. C. Lewis of Catskill, New York, the Rip Van Winkle was advertised as having, at the least, ''*twenty-seven* combinations, and by counting each recline or change of seat, back, or foot-rest, as other reclining or adjustable chair makers do, [it could] make over *two hundred* changes of position.'' It could be, at any given moment, a stationary or reclining easy chair, reclining rocker, reclining easy chair with tilted seat, platform or base rocker, rocker with foot-rest attached, settee, reclining couch, a cot six feet long, smoker's chair, and invalid's rolling chair ("the wheels can be removed in a minute and the chair is ready to go into your parlor"). Depending upon the choice of upholstery and finish, the price ranged from $20 to $35—and with doctor's gynecological attachment thrown in, the price was $40. In short, it was the ultimate chair, "The Most Wonderful Chair in the World," "A BEAUTIFUL Wedding or Holiday Present."[22]

85. The True Physiological Chair described and pictured in this Health Tract No. 13, issued c. 1865, was intended to rectify the conditions which bred consumption and spinal deformities. "That great barbarism, the unwieldy and disease-engendering rocking-chair," declared the writer, "favors these diseases and undoubtedly, in some instances, leads to bodily habits from which originate the ailments just named, to say nothing of piles, fistula and the like." With a short seat and fifth leg, the "physiological chair" accommodated the common position of tilting back in a straight chair.

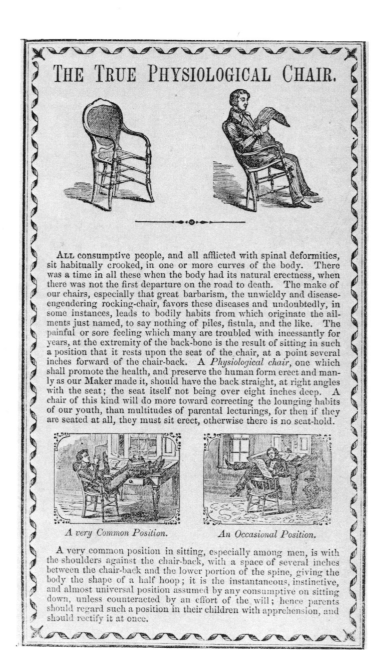

THE TRUE PHYSIOLOGICAL CHAIR.

ALL consumptive people, and all afflicted with spinal deformities, sit habitually crooked, in one or more curves of the body. There was a time in all these when the body had its natural erectness, when there was not the first departure on the road to death. The make of our chairs, especially that great barbarism, the unwieldy and disease-engendering rocking-chair, favors these diseases and undoubtedly, in some instances, leads to bodily habits from which originate the ailments just named, to say nothing of piles, fistula, and the like. The painful or sore feeling which many are troubled with incessantly for years, at the extremity of the back-bone is the result of sitting in such a position that it rests upon the seat of the chair, at a point several inches forward of the chair-back. A *Physiological chair*, one which shall promote the health, and preserve the human form erect and manly as our Maker made it, should have the back straight, at right angles with the seat; the seat itself not being over eight inches deep. A chair of this kind will do more toward correcting the lounging habits of our youth, than multitudes of parental lecturings, for then if they are seated at all, they must sit erect, otherwise there is no seat-hold.

A very Common Position. *An Occasional Position.*

A very common position in sitting, especially among men, is with the shoulders against the chair-back, with a space of several inches between the chair-back and the lower portion of the spine, giving the body the shape of a half hoop; it is the instantaneous, instinctive, and almost universal position assumed by any consumptive on sitting down, unless counteracted by an effort of the will; hence parents should regard such a position in their children with apprehension, and should rectify it at once.

Orville Cline

86. Swivel-rocker made at the Mt. Lebanon, New York, community of Shakers.

THE CELEBRATED RIP VAN WINKLE RECLINING ROCKING CHAIR.

Makes 15 Pieces of Furniture, and can be placed in 200 positions.

OVER.

87. Advertising card issued for the World's Columbian Exposition of 1893 and illustrating the Rip Van Winkle Reclining Rocking Chair made by the P.C. Lewis Manufacturing Company, Catskill, New York.

Rocking Chairs for Children

The needs of children were well-suited to the manipulations possible in patented convertible furniture. One of the most imaginative convertible rocking chairs, and certainly one of the earliest, the "Cradle-Chair," was patented by Samuel S. May in 1850. In the closed position, it was designed to look like a Boston rocking chair. When put to use as a cradle, one arm and pair of legs slid away from the seat, and the top two slats of the half-spindled chair back could be relocated in receiving holes along the front edge of the seat, or cradle bottom. May noted in his letters patent that "The chair is what is usually termed a rocking chair, or rests on rockers. They however may in some cases be dispensed with, in which case the article would more properly be termed a crib chair." Not only was this an ingenious space-saving invention, but it was also adaptable to the anti-rocking as well as the pro-rocking schools of child-rearing (figures 89 & 90).[23]

Several firms offered convertible highchairs. A few of these models could merely assume two positions, highchair and walker or carriage. One, included in the 1909 catalogue of the Bagby Furniture Company of Baltimore, Maryland, had no wheels for the carriage, but could become alternately a highchair or rocking chair. At least three other companies offered convertible children's chairs that could be held in three positions. In its tallest form, this unusual piece of furniture is a highchair with wheels. Midway in its descent to the ground, it can be fixed as a stroller or carriage. At its lowest point, with feeding tray removed, it becomes a rocking chair with elongated rockers.

The patented "Gem Chair," a version of the convertible highchair devised by Charles A. Perley of Baldwinsville, Massachusetts, in 1876 and advertised in C.W.H. Frederick's *Catalogue of Rattan, Reed, and Willow Ware*, could be had from their ware rooms on East Kinzie Street in Chicago for $6.50 each in 1883 (figure 88). Heywood

Brothers, who merged with the Wakefield Rattan Company in 1897 to become the still-productive Heywood-Wakefield Company of Gardner, Massachusetts, included a similar model in their catalogue of 1894. The popularity of the convertible highchair over a period of at least twenty years indicates that the type filled a middle-class need for multipurpose infant furniture. As separate pieces of apparatus, the highchair, stroller, and rocking chair occupied a good deal of space, while their real period of usefulness in the life of a child spanned a relatively short period of time. The storage area required to save each piece for the next child was reduced by two-thirds with the use of the convertible highchair.

The Glascock Brothers Manufacturing Company of Muncie, Indiana, offered another type of convertible furniture for infants with their "Baby Jumper and Rocking Chair," carrying both United

88. The "Gem Chair" produced by C.W.H. Frederick of Chicago was highchair, carriage, and rocker all in one. This example was offered for $6.50 in Frederick's *Catalogue of Rattan, Reed, and Willow Ware* of 1883.

No. 730. Gem Chair, as Rocker   As Carriage.   No. 730. As Chair.

89 & 90. May's convertible cradle-chair has the appearance of a Boston rocker when closed. To use as a cradle, one arm and pair of legs slide out and the top of the chair back becomes the cradle retainer. In his patent #7,418 of June 4, 1850, May suggested that it might also be made as a crib-chair without rockers. The few examples of this patented device which survive were probably made in the Sterling, Massachusetts, area where May lived.

91. Glascock's Baby Jumper and Rocking Chair as it appeared in a leaflet issued by the Glascock Brothers Manufacturing Company of Muncie, Indiana, around 1900.

States and Canadian patents issued between 1896 and 1898. The Glascocks' contribution to babies' comforts hung from a heavy frame by three large coiled springs. The perforated veneer-seat chair with footrest, restraining bar, and reclining back could swing freely or bounce up and down. When detached from the springs, rockers converted the swinging and bouncing seat to a conventional reclining rocking chair for infants. Indeed, this chair kept a baby exercised, entertained, napped, and perhaps fed throughout the day with a modicum of bending and moving on the part of the mother, who may not have had the wherewithal to hire a nursemaid for her children. The Glascocks' "Baby Jumper and Rocking Chair" could be both exercise chair and pacifier with a minimum of effort.

In the history of the rocking chair, the ingenious inventors of patented devices and attachments served two important functions. These enthusiastic tinkerers took the inherent motion of the rocking chair and set it to further useful services. But more important, the improvements they made upon the design and engineering of the simple rocker rendered it a welcome addition to most parlors. By the end of the nineteenth century, the rocking chair was at home in any room of the middle-class house. The proliferation of indoor models, however, did not decrease its use on that most necessary appendage of the Victorian home—the porch.

The Porch and the Rocking Chair

In the nineteenth century, the front porch was a place with its own specific rituals in the warmer months of the year. Whether open or enclosed, it was one of the cooler places in a house, especially in the early evening. As such, it became by the mid-nineteenth century an extension of the family sitting room. Children played upon it, friends were entertained within its boundaries, young lovers found it a cozy but respectable haven when other family members went about their evening retirement. Porches are not included on modern homes with as much frequency as they were in the nineteenth century because the porch no longer serves the evening social function it fulfilled in the past. A summer evening's home entertainment today is more likely to occur around the television set in the air-conditioned family room or around the barbecue pit on the back patio.

92. *Instructions for a Julep* by Newell Convers Wyeth (1882-1945).

93. Porch rockers, c. 1910.

94. In 1892, the Gendron Iron Wheel Company of Toledo, Ohio, offered this "Sewing Suit" in its catalogue of *Reed Furniture and Bamboo Novelties.*

Despite these modern alternatives, the porch remains an informal living space for many families, and the rocking chair has always been part of it in a variety of forms.

Because porches were an important informal family area for the home, they were included in the design of resort buildings in even larger proportions. Today, as in the past, large porches on vacation boarding houses and older un-air-conditioned resort hotels are stuffed with a veritable forest of rocking chairs. The danger to ambulatory movement when all are in use is enough to convince the nervous vacationer to sit down and relax.

Because of the resilient strength and the open patterns in which they can be woven, willow, reed, and rattan are suitable materials for porch furniture which is exposed to dust, rain, and changes in temperature not found inside the home (figure 97). The openwork of the weaving allows air to pass through to accommodate the front porch's environment as well as to provide a cooler seat. The flexible nature of the material makes it more responsive to body weight and movement than similar chairs made completely of wood. By the 1870s, suites of wicker, reed, and rattan porch furniture often included at least one rocking chair in the assembly, possibly a floor rocker or even the newer, more fashionable platform rocker. Expensive suites were nearly always woven in elaborate patterns that took further advantage of the thin dimensions and pliant nature of these materials.

95. Cover illustration for the 1878 *Price List of Rattan Furniture*, manufactured by the Wakefield Rattan Company, Boston.

97. *Below:* Wicker rockers were most appropriate for porches, but could also be used in informal family sitting rooms. This American model dates from the late nineteenth century.

96. *Above:* Wicker platform rocker, American, late nineteenth century.

105

98. Mary Elizabeth Rosencrantz and her doll near the porch of "The Hermitage," Ho-Ho-Kus, New Jersey, c. 1890.

Rustic Rockers

Informal vacation houses in the Adirondacks and other distant resort areas were often filled with rustic bentwood furniture. In this type of furniture, the decorative qualities of unfinished wood were emphasized—usually by keeping the bark, or at least twig scars, intact—although it was the flexible nature of thin branches that produced the vigorous and exciting profiles which rustic rockers exhibit (figure 99). Elaborate examples were made by individual craftsmen; the similarity of so many of the somewhat plainer sort, however, suggests that more than one manufacturer was involved in their production. Since the rustic look was acceptable in front porch furniture at home, the use of rustic rockers was not limited to vacation houses; nor was their

99. Bentwood rocking chair, American, c. 1900.

100. Plainer bentwood rockers were made by several firms in the East and, as is the case with this example, in the Midwest.

101. Some of the more elaborate bentwood rockers were probably made by individual craftsmen.

102. Made of a tree stump, and with a Windsor bow-back added, "the Chair of the President of the Chicago Convention" was a real novelty among rocking chairs and represented more the concept of rocker as throne, than rocker as comfortable seat. This illustration appeared in *Harper's Weekly*, May 19, 1860.

manufacture restricted to any one geographic area. For example, a reporter for the *American Agriculturist* magazine referred to a rustic bentwood rocking chair he had seen in St. Louis in 1871 as a ''Missouri Hoop-Pole Chair.''[24]

Rustic furniture was not always as exotic as the eccentric bentwood varieties might indicate. In the early twentieth century, the Old Hickory Chair Company of Martinsville, Indiana, produced a line of furniture in conventionally plain shapes made of uniform members with the bark left intact. Their ''old hickory'' furniture was advertised as being suitable for ''Roof Gardens, Summer and Rustic Homes, Verandas, Lawns, Dens, Studios, Snuggeries, Golf and Field Clubs.''[25]

Clearly, the second half of the nineteenth century was the most active period in the history of the rocking chair's design. Many of the manipulations performed on the rocking chair by inventors led, ultimately, to the platform or patent rocker—the most revolutionary change in the

103. ''Rockers with high backs are the most restful chairs for the porch,'' advised Alice M. Kellogg in *Home Furnishing* (1905), ''but a variety of styles should be chosen to suit different tastes.'' This porch in Wisconsin was furnished with plain, rustic, and Mission rockers to accommodate its many inhabitants. The photograph is dated September, 1913, and bears the invitation, ''will you be our Valentine?''

104. Advertisement of the Valley City Rattan Company, Grand Rapids, Michigan, from the *Michigan Artisan* of June, 1895.

105. Child-size models of the double rocker design are still available on today's market. This example was made about 1890 to accommodate very small dolls.

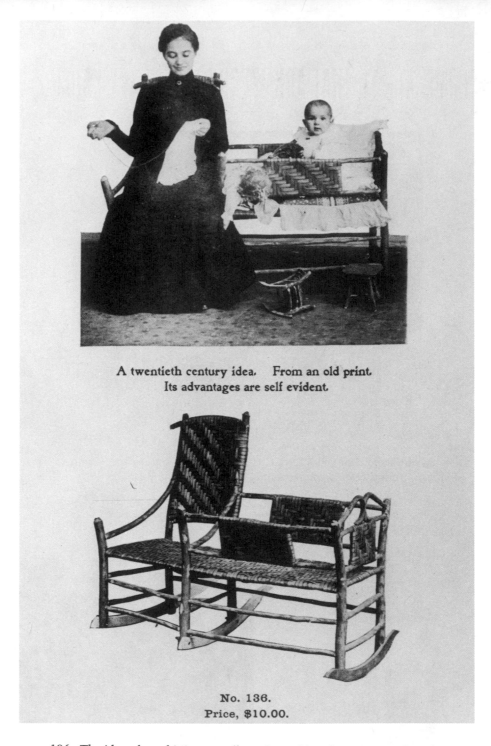

A twentieth century idea.   From an old print.
Its advantages are self evident.

No. 136.
Price, $10.00.

106. The idea of combining a cradle and a rocking chair in some form has
continued since the early nineteenth century. This rustic example was offered by the Old Hickory Chair Company of Martinsville, Indiana, in its
catalogue of 1901.

112

107. By the end of the nineteenth century, rocking was no longer the exclusive province of women, children and senior citizens.

design of the rocking chair during its history. The several upholstered varieties of floor rockers produced prior to 1850 were acceptable for some parlors; the complete disguise of the rockers, however, was the only way in which this unceremonious seat could ever hope to cross the sacred threshold permanently. Elaborate upholstery, long fringe, and a platform rendered the rocker indistinguishable from other parlor furniture.

At the opposite end of the continuum from platform rockers was Michael Thonet's bentwood rocking chair, another lasting innovation in rocker design. In addition to the physical pleasure it afforded, Thonet's design was the first to take advantage of the dramatic sculptural qualities inherent in the profile of the rocker itself. Whereas the platform concept meant to disguise the rockers, Thonet emphasized their elegantly active

line. Remarkably, both concepts are at least as popular today as they were in the Victorian period.

By the end of the nineteenth century, the rocking chair was fully integrated into the life-style of middle America and was gradually working its way into upper-class homes. Together with the innovation and variety that characterized this period existed a conservative desire for traditional types of rocking chairs. Ladder-back, Windsor, and Boston rockers continued to be made throughout the late nineteenth century, and, in fact, were offered in many of the same trade catalogues which featured the new styles. From its obscurity in the eighteenth century, the rocking chair had certainly become a ubiquitous seating form which could be made acceptable to every taste and situation.

108. Photograph of an unidentified woman, taken c. 1885. Sturdy rockers similar to this example are still produced.

4.
Something Old, Something New

At the same time that rocking chairs were manipulated to perform many comforting functions and were marketed to be a part of every middle-class parlor, many persons continued to prefer varieties of the early, standard rocking chair. Ladder-back rockers, Windsor-derived spindle-back rockers, and Boston rockers were manufactured throughout the latter half of the nineteenth century. The ease and relaxation derived from these relatively plain types of rocking chairs remained appealing to many rocker lovers despite the latest improvements dreamed up by motion engineers, tinkerers, and over-enthusiastic upholsterers. Several reasons for this situation are apparent, althouth the one that stands out most clearly is just plain tradition.

Shaker Rockers

Tradition in various forms was the hallmark of nineteenth-century Shaker communities, although their beginnings in the eighteenth century were somewhat less than traditional. The oldest communal organization in the United States, the Shakers originated in England as a small group of dissident Quakers under the direction of Ann Lee. Persecuted for their ideas regarding celibacy as well as for the shaking behavior which characterized their fervent worship, they left England permanently in 1774 to seek freedom in America.

After some initial problems with acceptance, they acquired a number of converts. Between 1787 and 1794, nine New England communities were organized. Eventually there would be a total of nineteen Shaker villages in New York, New Hampshire, Massachusetts, Connecticut, Ohio, Kentucky, and Indiana, although several were short-lived.

Above all, the Shakers believed in the values of clean living, industrious labor, and devotion to God. They made most of what they needed within

109. The gold slat-back rocker trademark of the Shaker's Mt. Lebanon, New York, chair industry guaranteed quality and durability of construction. The mark is on the inside of one rocker of the chair illustrated in figure 112.

110. Whether made for the community or the world outside, Shaker furniture is characterized by its plain elegance which came as a result of the group's sanctions against unnecessary ornament. This New Lebanon, New York, rocker was made between 1800 and 1830.

111. Meeting room with Shaker ladder-back and web-back rocking chairs arranged against the walls. From a photographic postcard, c. 1910.

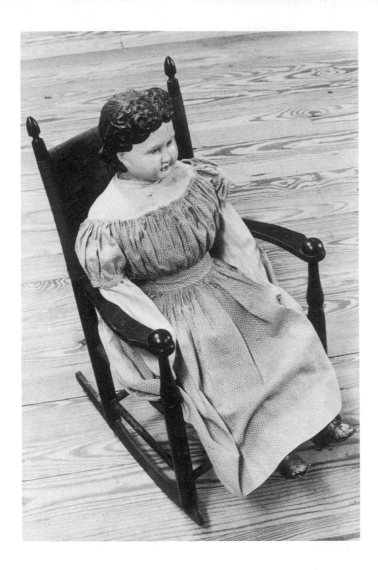

112. Shaker rockers were made in seven sizes. This child-size model ''0'' example, with worsted web seat and back, may have been made as late as 1930, since the design of Shaker rockers varied little over the sixty-five year period they were produced.

their communities and sold or traded other products to sustain their communal enterprise. The production of brooms and seeds and the manufacture of chairs were among their most profitable industries in tradable goods. They made all of their own furniture and so were competent cabinetmakers, but it was the chairs that they sold to the outside world.

Although the Shakers began to make and sell chairs for popular consumption in the late eighteenth century, not until 1863 did a member of the community survey both the market and the Shakers' production techniques with an eye towards marketability. In 1873, Brother Robert M. Wagan (1833-1883) reorganized the chairmaking industry at Mt. Lebanon, New York. Taking advantage of the principles of mass production, he separated chairmaking into its constituent parts, built new buildings, and acquired modern machinery. The new enterprise was known as ''R.M. Wagan & Company,'' and its label included as the central motif a three-slat rocking chair (figure 109).

Rocking chairs had of course been made by the

113. This Shaker ladder-back rocking arm-chair with worsted web seat is typical of those produced in the late nineteenth-century chair shops at Mt. Lebanon after Brother Wagan reorganized the Shaker Chair industry in 1873.

Shakers earlier in the nineteenth century, but, as with chairs in general, their production was haphazard. After the 1873 reorganization, the largest proportion of chairs made were rockers. Although regular arm and side chairs were offered for sale, only the rocking chairs were pictured prominently in their catalogues. All chairs were available in seven different sizes, ranging from the smallest child's size, which in the rocking chair had a seat of 12"x 10", to the largest adult size, 22"x 18½". Prices for rocking chair frames were each 25¢ more than its comparably sized stationary chair,

and ranged from $2.00 to $4.75 for those without arms, or $2.25 to $5.00 for those with arms.

Shaker commercial rocking chairs were offered in a narrow range of styles. The ladder-back rocking chair had, depending on size, three or four slats and an upholstered seat (figure 113). They sold for $3.50 to $8.50 with arms, and for $3.25 to $8.00 without arms. There were also rocking chairs with upholstered seats and backs which could, depending on the type of upholstery, cost as much as $9.00 more than those with upholstered seats alone. A rail at the top of the back for the attachment of a cushion could be included. It fitted onto the posts in place of the finials.

A limited variety of upholstery materials was available. Woven web seats and backs of worsted tape were the most common. The wool worsted tape was a durable upholstery material which was dyed any of fourteen different colors. Seats and backs were woven of a solid color or any combination of two colors. For a while, the Shakers wove their own tapes, but, by the time the chair industry was in full swing, they were buying the plain tape and dyeing it themselves. The Shakers also upholstered chairs in what they called "plush" or "shag," which looked very much like velvet. It was offered in scarlet, blue, or orange—each with black stripe—and in eleven solid colors. Plush was nearly twice as expensive as worsted web upholstery.

Although Brother Wagan died in 1883, the Shakers at Mt. Lebanon continued their chair business for another half-century until 1935. Because the chairmaking process had been organized as a mass-production operation, all chair parts were uniform within their respective sizes. Chairs were not made individually from beginning to end, because each Shaker craftsman was master of his or her own operation, just as is the case in the furniture industry today. Chair parts were stock-

114. Advertisement from *The Furniture Worker* of August 10, 1890.

115. The living room of the William H. Smith House, New Britain, Connecticut, 1900-15, illustrates that plain rockers were acceptable in rooms designed to be elegant. Two rockers at the lower right are probably Shaker products, both upholstered in plush. Bentwood rockers were developed in the Mt. Lebanon chair shops after the Centennial Exposition where Thonet Brothers exhibited its own famous bentwood rocker.

piled and used as needed. Once Brother Wagan put his newly-organized shop into operation in 1873, the Shakers' product did not change much. Thus, a chair made by the Shakers in 1930 is virtually indistinguishable from another made by them in 1880 or 1890.

There are no figures available on the number of rocking chairs made by the Shakers at Mt. Lebanon, but, over the sixty-two year period the

chair shop was in operation, there must have been many thousands turned out. Since these were not particularly inexpensive chairs, they generally found homes among the middle and upper classes. In its largest size, a plush upholstered Shaker rocker, for example, cost $17.50, nearly as much as M. & H. Schrenkeisen's medium-sized patent rocker no. 7 in "Terry, with stripe." The Shaker product, however, carried the prestige of the Mt. Lebanon community. Indeed, the Shakers had a reputation to uphold: their products were honest, well-made, and could be expected to last. Shaker chair catalogues always included an example of the trade mark and the assurance that it "will be attached to every genuine Shaker Chair...." "None others are of our make," such catalogues declared, "notwithstanding any claims to the contrary." The firm notice that "All persons are hereby cautioned not to use or counterfeit our Trade-Mark" suggests that similar chairs were made and marketed to compete, at least in appearance, with the famous Shaker product. That the Shaker rocker was in fact imitated may be seen in a price list of February 1, 1887, issued by the New Haven Folding Chair Company (with salesrooms in Chicago). Included as number 25, is a plush-seat-and-back arm rocker that had the appearance, and nearly the dimensions, of the largest Shaker rocker. Offered for $5.50, the imitation was much less expensive than its Shaker prototype.

116. "Then who shall dare to chide him for sticking to the Old Arm-Chair." The caption of this card advertising Van Stan's Stratena cement (c. 1885) is a slight corruption of a song by Eliza Cook and Henry Russell, published in 1840 but popular for many years. The song is a sentimental ode to a mother's old chair. Here, however, the rocking chair and verse emphasize that the product is a time-honored standard.

Although the Shakers were certainly among the major proponents of tradition in America in the late nineteenth century, by no means did they have a corner on the market. The taste for plain rocking chairs was evident in the catalogues and advertisements of many furniture firms. The Warren Chair Works, of Warren, Pennsylvania, "manufacturers of dining, plain and fancy chairs and a high grade of rockers," pictured a ladder-back rocker with plush seat in their advertisement in the *Furniture Worker* of August 10, 1890 (figure 117). There are details on this chair that identify it with the late nineteenth century. The basic idea, however—a ladder-back rocker with cushion—is unchanged from the eighteenth century.

Updated versions of the Windsor chair were also offered to ready consumers in the late nineteenth century (figure 120). Although these were covered with ornament suitably designed for the period, and exhibited more turnings than would have appeared on any eighteenth century example, spindle-back chairs are essentially descendants of the earlier types. Made in oak or elm and finished to a high gloss, these chairs were common to most middle-class American homes.

In addition to the desire for rocking chairs in the plain eighteenth-century style, there existed an uninterrupted taste for the clean lines of the late Empire Grecian style. Cane seat-and-back nurse rockers continued to be made singly and as part of bedroom suites. Clarence Cook in his 1877 essay on *The House Beautiful* advised that "The wooden chairs, and chairs seated with rushes or cane of the old time, were as comfortable as the

117. Despite the obvious attempt to "modernize" this chair with eccentric turnings and shallow machine-carved surface decoration, it is still obviously a ladder-back rocker. Advertised in *The Furniture Worker* for August 10, 1890.

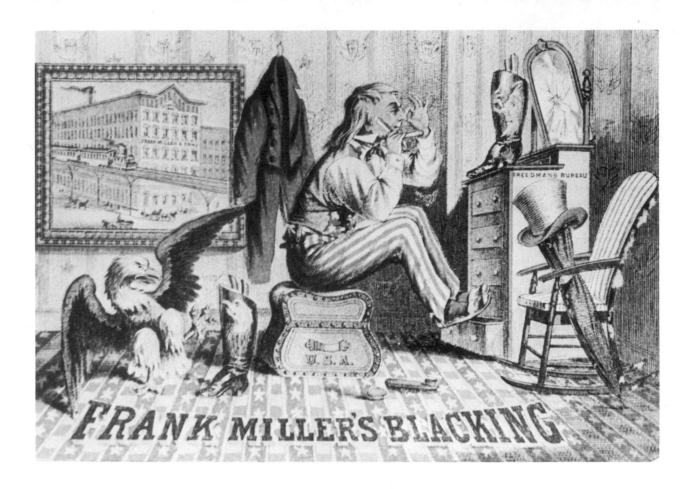

118. *Above:* Frank Miller & Sons would have the consumer believe that its boot blacking was as American as Uncle Sam, the eagle, and the rocking chair. Advertising card by Mayer, Merkel & Ottman, New York, c. 1885.

119. Henry Zabriski of Hawthorne, New Jersey, made this child's rocker for the Demerest family of Bergen County about 1850. Without documentary evidence to the contrary, it could easily be dated fifty years earlier.

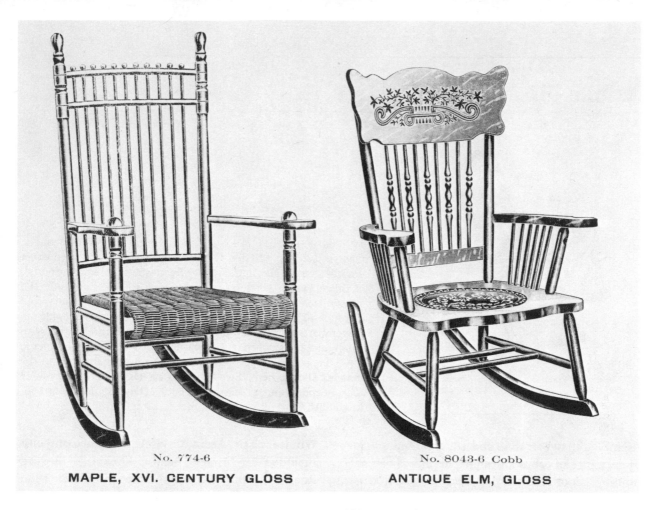

No. 774-6
MAPLE, XVI. CENTURY GLOSS

No. 8043-6 Cobb
ANTIQUE ELM, GLOSS

120. Many chair manufacturing firms offered rockers which displayed traditional antecedents to varying degrees. "Gloss" is the shiny varnish finish typical of furniture from this period. From the 1896 catalogue of Walter Heywood, New York.

stuffed and elastic seats we are so fond of. And if we could consent to come back to something of the old-fashioned austerity, we should find it greatly to our profit in many ways." In 1886, C. N. Arnold and Company of Poughkeepsie, New York, offered the "Plain Nurse, No Arm" and "French Arm Nurse" with suggestive half-arms, as well as Grecian "Scroll Arm" rockers with saw-cut sabre or lathe-turned straight front legs. The same *Illustrated Catalogue of Chairs* included the more fashionable "Queen Anne Sewing Rocker," "Grant Sewing Rocker," "Bamboo Reception Rocker," "Victoria Spindle Sewing Rocker," and "Eastlake Cane Back Sewing Rocker," as well as a variety of cane seat-and-back platform and pedestal-base spring rockers.

William Moore, a cabinetmaker who immigrated to Pennsylvania from County Roscommon in Ireland, kept a sketchbook now in the collection of the Athenaeum of Philadelphia. The book,

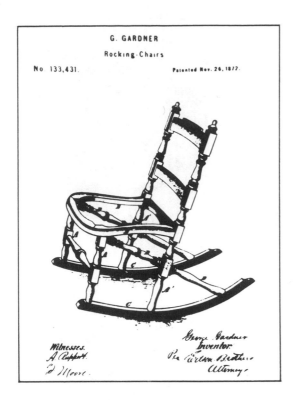

121. Although best known for his perforated veneer seats, George Gardner, of Glen Gardner, New Jersey, patented other devices as well. He claimed that "by means of bracing the parts" of this elaborate version of the slat-back rocker, "not only is a substantial chair furnished, but one possessing beauty and elegance of appearance." He was granted patent #133,431 on November 26, 1872. Several other rocking chairs are known with small braces between the back legs and rockers. Gardner's, however, is the only rocking chair with braces arranged in the manner shown here. Swedish rocking chairs have very long rockers and two extra legs in the back. They should not be confused with Gardner's patented brace rocker.

assembled between 1848 and 1897, includes careful drawings of cabinet designs, details of cabinet moldings, door construction, and veneer patterns, all with relevance to his line of work. Mixed within these careful drawings are sketches of only a few chairs (after all, he was a cabinetmaker), and most of these are rocking chairs. Evidently the form struck his fancy, for none of the sketches refer exactly to the details of known rocking chairs. On the other hand, over two-thirds of the examples are variations on the Grecian style, plain or with extra flourishes. If Moore, whose cabinetwork was in the various historical styles popular in the late nineteenth century, continued to think of the rocking chair in terms of the Grecian style, then there were probably others around him in Philadelphia of the same mind.

Because of its curves in the seat and back, the Boston rocker fits into this same Grecian-style group even though it derives essentially from the Windsor chair. Again, C. N. Arnold and Company included a "Misses' Boston Rocker," "Boston Rocker," and "Boston Nurse" in their 1886 catalogue. These chairs mimicked the original versions of the 1830s. Clearly taste for the old styles and types existed alongside taste for the fashionable. In some cases manufacturers and retailers capitalized on the conservative and nostalgic turn of mind. Butler Brothers, a Chicago firm, carried "OLD FASHIONED ROCKING CHAIRS" in their 1891-92 catalogue, *Specialities in Furniture*. These were essentially Boston rocking chairs, but without the roll up in the back. The spindle-back version "Flat Seat Rocker—The good old-fashioned pattern which never goes out of favor"—was listed at $3.10, a small price to pay for a visual link to the past. Flat seat rocker number 170, with a vase-shaped back splat, was highly recommended because "no more popular or steadier selling chair than this is made," and it cost only $3.20 each.

122. Although wealthy urban families were slow to incorporate rocking chairs into adult furnishings for their public rooms, children nearly always had them. The plain child's rocking chair in the lower left of Eastman Johnson's engaging portrait of *The Family of Alfredrick Smith Hatch in Their Residence at Park Avenue and 37th Street, New York City* (1871) could have been made almost any time during the nineteenth century.

123. Although the display techniques used in this Black River Falls, Wisconsin, furniture store, photographed at the turn of the century by Charles Van Schaick, are more informal than those of today, the customer could still survey the wares these gentlemen offered. The ceiling is a forest of spindle-back rockers and chairs.

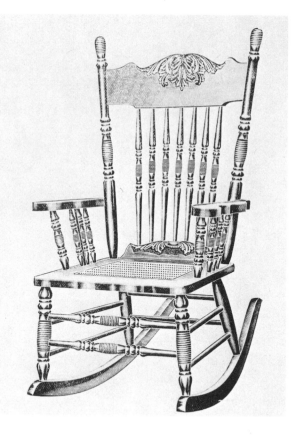

124. Elaborate spindle-back chairs in oak and elm were popular in the late nineteenth and early twentieth centuries. Although they have more turned decoration on stretchers, legs, and spindles, they are, nonetheless, descendants of the older, plainer versions. Ornament steam-pressed into the top slat replaced the stenciled or painted patterns of their ancestors. As in the past, chairs were made with and without arms. From the 1896 catalogue of Walter Heywood, New York.

BROAD ARM ROCKER.

No. 32.—Walnut.　　Rub Finish.　　Cane or Perforated.
No. 132.—Maple.　　Walnut Finish.　　Cane or Perforated.

47

125 & 126. Rocking chairs with cane seats and backs in the Grecian style were marketed throughout the nineteenth century in forms similar to the originals of the 1830s. The straight front legs and small turned elements in the backs of these two examples identify them with the late nineteenth century. The illustrations are from the G. Stomps and Company (Dayton, Ohio) catalogue of 1887 and the Marietta Chair Company (Marietta, Ohio) catalogue of 1889-90.

127. "Fourth of July—Nowadays," *Harper's Weekly*, July 4, 1860. By 1860, the old Revolutionary War hero could relax during the celebration of the independence he had helped to make a reality. The Boston rocker in which he sits was so common that it had become a standard symbol of the American way of life by the mid-nineteenth century.

One Home Through Time

Tracing the appearance and disappearance of rocking chairs within a particular home over time yields evidence of patterns of taste, usage, and behavior. Cherry Hill, the home for two centuries of a Van Rensselaer family in Albany, New York, is only one example. Although the evidence in this case gives a somewhat interrupted look at only the last 150 years of occupation, it is dramatic. An inventory taken at the death of Solomon Van Rensselaer in 1852 indicates that Cherry Hill at that time housed only one rocking chair (valued at 25¢) in the "North West Bed Room" which also contained a carpet, rug, oilcloth, window curtains and shades, stove, fireboard, gilt frame looking glass, bedroom crockery, six black chairs, eight pictures, but no bed. Photographs taken about 1880 show that at least four, and possibly seven, rockers were in use in the dining room, library, and three bedrooms (figure 135). Today, the house remains largely the way it was left by its last

128. The rocking chair was often used by cartoonists to suggest laziness when able-bodied men were the occupants. "The Man Who Doesn't," as pictured in *Harper's Weekly* for July 4, 1857, is pitched back in his chair in an unpatriotic manner, for this is the lazy way he chose to observe Independence Day.

owner in 1963. Photographs taken of the same rooms in the house in 1973 show no rocking chairs at all. All of the rocking chairs visible in the 1880 photographs were of the plainer varieties—cane seat-and-back sewing rockers and Shaker rockers—and were added to the house sometime before the photographs were taken.[1]

Solomon Van Rensselaer was 88 years old when he died in 1852; his wife Arriet had died in 1840. Either they had had no use for more than one plain rocking chair, or the others did not survive. Or perhaps the Van Rensselaers never used their rocker personally, but had it available for the children's nurse. The inventory really gives no clues as to use, only location in this case.

Harriet Maria, Solomon's daughter, and her husband, the physician Peter Elmendorf, occupied the house after Solomon's death and seem to represent the generation which added the largest number of rocking chairs to Cherry Hill's furniture holdings. Their interest in them was something other than their importance for the nursery, however, since their two children had already entered middle childhood by the time the family occupied the house. Perhaps they all enjoyed rocking, since rocking chairs were located in all the bedrooms. And by the third quarter of the nineteenth century, of course, rocking chairs had become necessary bedroom furniture. As one might expect, neither parlor seemed to have rocking chairs, which would tend to substantiate the assumption that rocking chairs were generally considered too informal to be included in many formal rooms. That a cane seat-and-back rocking chair was included in the Elmendorf dining room indicates, of course, that this room was con-

129. "Old Fashioned Rocking Chairs" offered by Butler Brothers in the firm's *Specialties in Furniture* catalogue of 1891-92.

130. Demand for pure Boston rockers did not abate by the late nineteenth century. The "Pittsburgh" rocker, a type derived from the Boston rocker but with a horseshoe-shaped back, was made primarily in western Pennsylvania and eastern Ohio, including the German Pietist community at Zoar, Tuscarawas County. The illustrations are from the Marietta Chair Company catalogue for 1889-90.

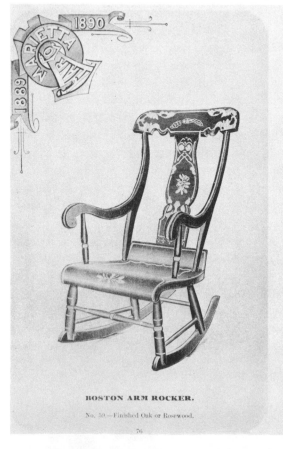

BOSTON ARM ROCKER.

No. 59.—Finished Oak or Rosewood.

76

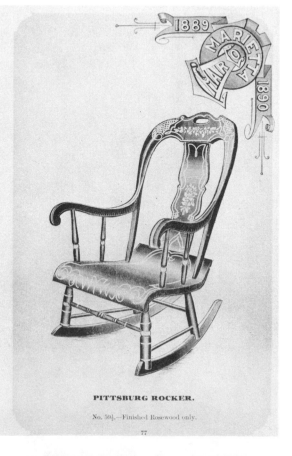

PITTSBURG ROCKER.

No. 59½.—Finished Rosewood only.

77

131. *Sitting by the Hearth*, painted by Harry Roseland in 1899.

sidered somewhat more informal than the parlor. Day beds or lounges, in fact, were often located in or recommended for dining rooms in the eighteenth and nineteenth centuries, a fact that will surprise most readers. Ella Rodman Church in her advice on *How to Furnish a Home* (1883) suggested that "A lounge to match the chairs is a pleasant addition to the furniture of the dining room; it should not, however, be fluffy or billowy in shape, but rather of a classic and severe expression." If, then, a lounge was considered "proper,"

why not a rocker? The Elmendorfs' use of rocking chairs in the library is also consistent with tradition. After all, Benjamin Franklin had one in his, and the library is surely a room in which one might relax.

Between 1860 and 1875 the numbers and types of rocking chairs manufactured increased greatly. The Elmendorfs did not choose to include some of the more elaborate forms available by the 1870s, but tended toward the more traditional plain forms. Evidence that they included more rocking

132. *Telling the News*, painted by John George Brown in the late nineteenth century. With his feet propped high and a cushion for his head, this man enjoys his daily newspaper while relaxing in a Boston rocker. He has removed his glasses to recount or remark upon something he has read, just as Mrs. Nicholas Salisbury had a century earlier from her easy chair (figure 9). Unlike the painting of Mrs. Salisbury, however, this is not a portrait made to preserve the likeness of a particular person of wealth. It is more accurately described as genre painting, a class of art which depicts a typical aspect of everyday life. John George Brown (1831-1913), who excelled as a genre painter, recorded the luxuries indulged in by elderly men of rural New England during this period—a comfortable rocking chair and the free expression of opinion. The accoutrements of wealth gathered around Mrs. Salisbury have been replaced by the intimate paraphernalia of an old man's daily life—comb, brush, shaving mug, mirror, scissors, hat, and cane—arranged across the background.

133. In this advertisement for "Glascock's Improved Invalid Table" (c. 1900), the rocker is still associated with the comfort of the infirm.

134. The late-nineteenth-century painted decoration and rustic materials used in this example, which appeared in the *Michigan Artisan* of June 1884, do not disguise the fact that its basic form with rolled seat and scrolled arms was derived from the Boston rocker.

135. Dining Room at Cherry Hill, Albany, New York, photographed about 1880. Furniture of a comfortable nature, such as the couch and rocking chair shown here, is not normally included in modern dining rooms. In seventeenth- and eighteenth-century homes, dining was only one activity which occurred in the parlor, so furnishings were varied and versatile. This carried over to some degree into the nineteenth century. Even though most homes included separate parlors and dining rooms, the latter often contained a couch or daybed, a provision recommended in the leading decorating manuals of the period. The medallion cane-seat-and-back rocking chair was a typical inexpensive model made between 1850 and 1875 in both England and America.

Sinclair's Reading and Writing Table for Chairs.
⁓ IMPROVED. ⁓

DIRECTIONS FOR USING.—Sit in the Chair, placing the table across the arms; catching the hook under inside edge of right arm, bring moveable button at right hand near the arm, handle to front; bring handle to rear, which secures the table to the chair. Table swings on pivot so it can be left on chair if desired.

Size for Nos. 4, 13 and 16 Chair, 32x16 inches.

Weight of Table, only Six Pounds.

F. A. Sinclair's Reading and Writing Table for Chairs is adjustable to nearly all kinds of ARM chairs; can be set any angle desired; is a great convenience in reading a heavy book, or for writing purposes; and makes a good cutting or lap board for ladies. Also, dining table for invalids.

Walnut Table, without chair			$3 50
"	"	ornamented without chair	4 00
"	"	Chess Board in centre, without chair	4 50

136. During the 1880s, F. A. Sinclair of Mottville, New York, advertised his ''American Common Sense Rockers'' in England. Rocking chairs, he declared, were ''to be found in every American home, and no family [could] keep house without them.'' In this illustration from Sinclair's catalogue of 1882, the gentleman is seated in a standard ''Old Puritan Rocker,'' available ''in vermilion'' for $6.50.

chairs in furnishing their home reflects the increased usage of rocking chairs among the population in general. On the other hand, the inclusion of rockers of the plainer sort echoes the nostalgia for the past that began to creep into notions of furnishing during this period, as well as the oft-repeated recommendations for chairs of plain, sturdy construction in the decorating books. In consciously choosing to preserve the past at Cherry Hill, the Elmendorfs added very little to the furniture accumulation of the four preceding generations. The addition of plain rocking chairs, was, in fact, a nostalgic homage to the past.

Rocking chairs were not really included in the decorating scheme developed by Mrs. Rankin, the last member of the Van Rennselaer family to occupy the house, probably because only one rocking chair was in use prior to 1850. Mrs. Rankin's scheme of interior decoration was a historical one—a plan based on the old pieces of furniture that had survived in the house—and her choices tended to follow the types and styles of furniture introduced to the house before 1850. Thus, the inclusion of rocking chairs in her plan would have been inappropriate.

The survival of a house such as Cherry Hill, with much of its history and contents intact, does indeed provide useful evidence towards our understanding of the rocking chair in the nineteenth and early twentieth centuries. The Elmendorfs, in par-

137. *A Family Group* by an unknown artist, watercolor, c. 1875.

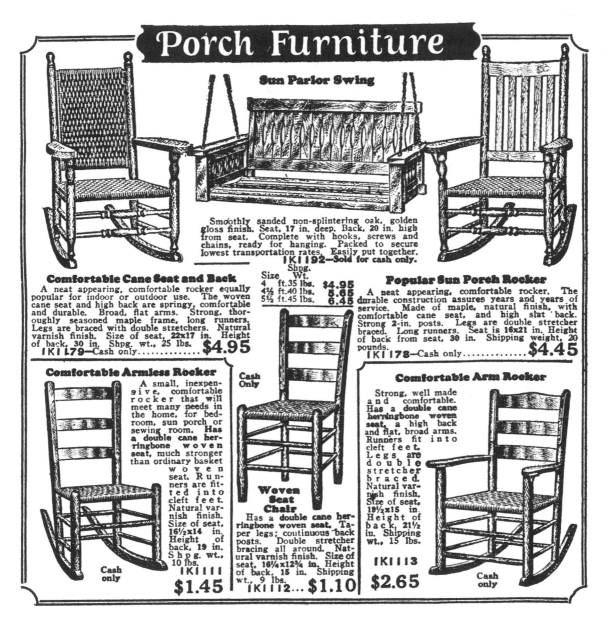

Porch Furniture

Sun Parlor Swing

Smoothly sanded non-splintering oak, golden gloss finish. Seat, 17 in. deep. Back, 20 in. high from seat. Complete with hooks, screws and chains, ready for hanging. Packed to secure lowest transportation rates. Easily put together.
1K1192—Sold for cash only.

Size	Shpg. Wt.	
4 ft.	35 lbs.	$4.95
4½ ft.	40 lbs.	5.65
5½ ft.	45 lbs.	6.45

Comfortable Cane Seat and Back

A neat appearing, comfortable rocker equally popular for indoor or outdoor use. The woven cane seat and high back are springy, comfortable and durable. Broad, flat arms. Strong, thoroughly seasoned maple frame, long runners. Legs are braced with double stretchers. Natural varnish finish. Size of seat, 22x17 in. Height of back, 30 in. Shpg. wt., 25 lbs.
1K1179—Cash only............. **$4.95**

Popular Sun Porch Rocker

A neat appearing, comfortable rocker. The durable construction assures years and years of service. Made of maple, natural finish, with comfortable cane seat, and high slat back. Strong 2-in. posts. Legs are double stretcher braced. Long runners. Seat is 16x21 in. Height of back from seat, 30 in. Shipping weight, 20 pounds.
1K1178—Cash only............. **$4.45**

Comfortable Armless Rocker

A small, inexpensive, comfortable rocker that will meet many needs in the home, for bedroom, sun porch or sewing room. Has a double cane herringbone woven seat, much stronger than ordinary basket woven seat. Runners are fitted into cleft feet. Natural varnish finish. Size of seat, 16½x14 in. Height of back, 19 in. Shpg. wt., 10 lbs.
1K1111
Cash only
$1.45

Woven Seat Chair

Cash Only

Has a double cane herringbone woven seat. Taper legs; continuous back posts. Double stretcher bracing all around. Natural varnish finish. Size of seat, 16¼x12¾ in. Height of back, 15 in. Shipping wt., 9 lbs.
1K1112... **$1.10**

Comfortable Arm Rocker

Strong, well made and comfortable. Has a double cane herringbone woven seat, a high back and flat, broad arms. Runners fit into cleft feet. Legs are double stretcher braced. Natural varnish finish. Size of seat, 19½x15 in. Height of back, 21½ in. Shipping wt., 15 lbs.
1K1113
Cash only
$2.65

138. Ostensibly regarded as "porch furniture," these plain rockers were advertised in the 1927 Sears, Roebuck catalogue as "equally popular for indoor or outdoor use." The armless rocker at the lower left would "meet many needs in the home, for bedroom, sun porch or sewing room." These simple rocking-chair types, made continuously since the eighteenth century, illustrate that the original concept was one which would not be completely altered by fashion. Durability, neatness, and comfort are the enduring attributes of the common rocker.

139. Only death would ultimately separate Beata Krans (1811-1899) from her crocheting and her bow-back Windsor rocking chair. Her son Olof Krans (1838-1916) painted from memory many portraits and scenes of life around Bishop Hill, Illinois, a colony of Swedish religious dissenters founded by Eric Jansen and Jonas Olson in 1846. Organized along communistic lines, the community was dissolved formally in 1862, although the village and several of the original buildings are still extant.

140. *John Presents The Monthly Gas Tax*. "Paterfamilias: 'Well, John, just in proportion as the quality of the gas goes down, the size of the bills goes up.'" Sturdy, wide arm rockers were used in parlors as well as on porches, although in this instance the cartoonist has included it to emphasize his message that a modern improvement may not be as reliable as the "old-fashioned" way. The conversions from candle and kerosene light to gas did present problems to home owners in the 1880s. *Harper's Weekly* for May 14, 1881.

ticular, represent the complexity of some of the cultural forces which surrounded the acceptance, use, and design of the rocking chair. In this case, the desire for personal comfort was defined within a conservative attitude toward the appearance of an artifact. This same conservative turn of mind, in fact, perpetuated the traditional character of the rocking chair's design during a period when many new styles were offered.

By the late nineteenth century, the rocking chair had in many ways undergone tremendous change from the concept of a common chair with rockers added which had prevailed in 1800. Since those early days, it had been decorated, upholstered, and patented beyond recognition, but it had also, in many respects, remained virtually the same. New rocking chair styles emerged during the twentieth century, although the year 1900 was certainly no watershed of radical changes. The Art Nouveau movement, which occupied the interest of wealthy style-conscious Europeans, never touched the rocking chair's design except for a few extra flourishes added to Thonet's bentwood rocker. Pressed and spindled oak rockers, plain cane seat-and-back varieties, upholstered floor and platform designs, and common Windsor and slat-back rocking chairs continued to be popular in homes where a desire for comfort prevailed over the need to be fashionable. The rocking chair had become a standard requirement for many homes. Its appearance evolved after 1900 as it was adapted to new styles and sensibilities, but, in general, the varieties of the rocking chair form which developed during the nineteenth century were carried deep into the twentieth century as well.

141. Norman Dicken, photographed at the Dicken Photographic Studio, Fostoria, Ohio, c. 1915.

5.
From Quaint to Colonial

In the beginning of the twentieth century a "Craftsman Movement" resulted in a kind of revolution in furniture design. As in earlier nineteenth-century art reform movements, the devotion of its adherents was virtually religious. They felt a satisfaction with the simplicity and careful craftsmanship exhibited in the purest examples of the furniture made in what the popular press later called the "Mission" style. The inspiration for the new movement was inaccurately described in the Grand Rapids *Furniture Record* about 1910:

> It is undeniable that the people of today desire their furniture plain, the popularity of the California and the so-called Mission effects furnishing abundant evidence of this taste. The severely simple, yet graceful and utilitarian appearing Mission, may be a fad as some critics affect to believe, yet it is certain to leave its impression on the furniture styles of the future.

> Mission furniture is really rather a type than a style. Its origin, as the name would imply, is in the early Spanish California missions of the Jesuits. An old chair and settee from an ancient mission house, secured by a collector of odd and antique furniture, furnished the inspiration of the style.[1]

Surprisingly, the origins of the Mission furniture industry lay to the East, in England, rather than in the western missions of California. As early as the middle of the nineteenth century, such English writers as John Ruskin and Charles Lock Eastlake advocated moral integrity in production and functional and honest design. The Aesthetic Movement, and later the Arts and Crafts Movement, as it became known in England and in the United States, glorified the craftsmanship of the individual and rejected the sterile and mechanical aspects of factory production.[2]

These efforts to improve the quality of life by fostering a renewed appreciation of handiworks were soon noticed in the United States. Many people in such large cities as Boston, Minneapolis, New York, and Chicago formed societies or guilds for the arts and crafts, and exhibitions throughout the country displayed the latest designs of local artist-craftsmen. The attraction to the aesthetic way of life was strong enough to engender whole communities of talented woodworkers, metalsmiths, book designers, potters, and others.

Stickley's Craftsman Style

One of the most influential furniture designer-manufacturers of this period was Gustave Stickley. His earliest furniture, made in partnership with various relatives, ranged typically from fancy and eclectic to Colonial in inspiration. By 1898, he had formed the Gustave Stickley Company in Eastwood, a suburb of Syracuse, New York, and commenced production of the plain, substantial oak furniture that was to influence so many of America's manufacturers (figure 143). It soon

142. The brothers Charles and Henry Greene were trained in St. Louis in the manual arts by Calvin Woodward, who had been strongly influenced by John Ruskin and William Morris. After schooling in classical architecture at the Massachusetts Institute of Technology, the Greenes became fascinated with the argicultural landscape and Spanish missions of southern California and settled into practice as architects in Pasadena before 1900. Oriental arts and the words and work of Gustav Stickley had a profound influence on their designs in 1901. Although the Greenes included Stickley's furniture in their houses in 1902, they were creating their own furniture designs by 1903. This inglenook and rocking chair are part of the house and furnishings designed for Mr. & Mrs. David B. Gamble in 1908.

143. This ladies' sewing rocker of quarter-sawn white oak with a leather seat was produced at the Craftsman Workshops of Gustav Stickley, c. 1910.

144. Red decal mark used on the Craftsman furniture of Gustav Stickley, who advertised that "The value of a device is universally recognized. Obedient to this time-honored principle, the workmen of the United Crafts are constantly stimulated by the Flemish motto first used by Jan van Eyck, and later, in French translation, adopted by William Morris. The 'If I can' is an incentive to the craftsman who seeks to advance the cause of art allied to labor."

145. Gustav Stickley arm rocker, quarter-sawn American white oak, c. 1905. "As an American by birth, I chose to work with native growths. I felt the possibilities of our forest products to be great, and I wished to experiment with them." So wrote Stickley in *The Craftsman* (October, 1904).

became necessary to adopt a distinctive trade mark to distinguish his own "Craftsman" furniture from that of his brothers, Leopold and J. George, who had left his workshop in 1900 to form a rival company in Fayetteville, New York. A decal with a joiner's compass and the words "Als ik kan" (If I can) called attention to Stickley's philosophy of the craftsman aesthetic (figure 144). In a 1910 *Craftsman* article, Stickley reminisced about the past:

> When we began to make the Craftsman furniture, it was with the idea of getting the minds of the people away from the bad habit of demanding a ceaseless stream of "novelties" in the way of personal belongings and household furnishings. It seemed to us that these belongings were essentially a part of our lives and must needs bear an important share in the creation of that environment which psychologists tell us

has so much to do with the formation of character. Therefore, it seemed clear that we could hardly spend too much thought or care in the designing and making of the things we were to live with and use every day, seeing to it that these things were first of all truthful; that is, that they were made in the shape which would give them the greatest usefulness and durability combined with the utmost simplicity. If this principle were sincerely carried out, they must inevitably be beautiful because, in the very nature of things, there could be nothing vulgar or artificial about them.[3]

Although popular articles on so-called Mission furniture played upon its coincidental resemblances to the early oak furniture of Spanish California, Stickley's Craftsman furniture was actually inspired by early Japanese and unadorned Gothic models. Other manufacturers adapted his

146. Leopold and J. George Stickley were brothers of Gustav Stickley and left his workshop in 1900 to form a rival furniture company. Their products, like this oak Mission armchair rocker, c. 1908-1912, were cheaper imitations of the more famous "Craftsman" furniture.

ideas for mass production so that the average consumer could purchase the desired fashion. Only then did the press mythicize the mission source.

Several rocking chairs were available from the Craftsman Workshops of Gustav Stickley, including armchair and sewing rockers (figure 145). Invariably made of well-chosen quarter-sawn white oak, they featured leather or rush seats. As in much of the best Mission-style furniture, the construction openly displayed mortise and tenon and peg joints to emphasize the handmade aspect of its craft. Honesty and durability in construction was the Stickley maxim and veneered surfaces or nailed and glued joints were anathemas. A magazine writer noted in 1909 that "The Mission is in many respects an admirable style—straight, simple and solid. If, as has been facetiously said, it was designed to withstand the frequent earthquake shocks of southern California, still, with

proper surroundings, it is a most satisfactory object to look upon and—when the particular Mission is a chair or settee—to sit upon."[4]

Not content to manufacture the increasingly popular Craftsman furniture, Stickley and others ambitiously sought to reform interior decoration and later to suggest plans for houses suitable to their designs. Soon, Craftsman bungalows appeared all over the country. The houses were modern in a plain, "quaint" way, and one of the victims of their introduction was the parlor, to be replaced by the living room. An editorial in the *Savannah (Georgia) News* of the early 1900s took note of its disappearance:

How vividly the picture of the old fashioned parlor comes back to mind! There was the mohair covered sofa; the mohair covered rocking chair and the mohair covered standing chairs all shiny, very slick and very comfort-

147

able. The chairs stood as straight as if their perpendicular had been determined with a plumb line and their seats were springy and bulbous. The small boy who attempted to sit on one of them found himself perpetually slipping off and then crawling back on again. In one corner was the what-not, an ornate affair on which were gathered cups and saucers bearing such legends as "For a Good Boy," "For a Good Girl," "To Our Mother" and the like, in addition to a hundred gewgaws and jim-cracks defying description.[5]

Mission Furniture

If the parlor was a vanishing vestige of Victoriana, the rocking chair most certainly was not. Most of the furniture manufacturers who followed Stickley's lead in design, if not in quality, included several examples of rockers in their catalogues. Leopold and J. George Stickley, younger brothers of Gustav, often adapted his designs for production at their nearby factory in Fayetteville, New York (figure 146). Again, quarter-sawn white oak was the primary wood in chairs, although veneer was sometimes used to cut costs on larger case pieces. In Grand Rapids, Michigan, still more Stickley brothers, George and Albert, found Gustav's success difficult to ignore and set out to market an entire line of "Quaint Furniture" in the Mission style (figure 147).

Many other companies manufactured rocking chairs in Mission designs, but the results varied greatly as to quality of design and construction. Some popular magazines of the period published drawings for do-it-yourself craftsmen to put meaning into the handiwork ethic. The simplistic patterns allowed for little creativity, but a modicum of satisfaction in following Stickley's dictum of handcraft:

> We have advocated the restoration of handicrafts,—not because we have any quarrel with machinery as such, but because we believe that the ideals and standards resulting from thoughtless extravagance in the mechanical production of things are the cause of most of the evil that has fastened itself upon our national life. Therefore, we urge a return to the standards of work which prevailed in the days of handicrafts, because the only means we have of getting interest and joy out of what we do in every department of life lies in the training of that most sensitive and wonderful instrument, the human hand, to express the images conceived in the brain.[6]

At least one enterprising industrialist founded the Come-Packt Furniture Company in Ann Arbor, Michigan, whose 1910 catalogue featured mail-

147. This metal label tacked under the seat of the Stickley Brothers Company rocking chair identifies it as having been made sometime after 1905 when the words *"Quaint" Furniture* were added to the firm's advertising.

148. Mission furniture had the solid, simple beauty that enabled it to mix well with rustic interiors of hunting lodges and mountain resorts. Rocking chairs were always included to ensure the comfort of vacationers.

order Mission furniture packed for easy assembly. All that was necessary to furnish the bungalow were some nails or screws and a finish of one's choice.

Sturdiness and simplicity enabled Mission furniture to be used in a wide range of settings from the bedroom to the hunting lodge. Often given a fumed or weathered oak finish, it was appropriate in many informal situations. Mission rocking chairs could be found on porches, in summer cabins, and at seaside resorts—in fact, wherever plain comfort was appreciated. The style blended well with rustic interiors and its simple virtues enabled it to be used with many other styles of furnishings (figure 148).

One of the most interesting characters involved in creating Mission furniture was Charles Rohlfs who began as an industrial designer of cast-iron stoves and later became a well-known Shakespearean actor. After 1890 Rohlfs was involved in small-scale production of original, often custom-designed furniture. He displayed work at the Pan American Exposition of 1901, the Exhibition of Modern Decorative Arts in Turin, Italy, in 1902, and at the St. Louis World's Fair in 1904. Some of his designs in oak were plain enough to share the appellation ''Mission,'' although at his small workshop in Buffalo he frequently found that rectilinear style too confining, and carved sensuous Art Nouveau patterns into the broad surfaces. His workshop mark was an ''R'' enclosed in the rectangular frame of a saw, with the date sometimes added below. One novelty which Rohlfs designed was a rocking stool, the top upholstered in leather, meant to be used in conjunction with his rocking chairs. Few other manufacturers have realized the suitability of a footstool which rocks.

The beautiful Mission furnishings were eventually to give way to new styles provided by manufacturers who, no doubt, feared that the substan-

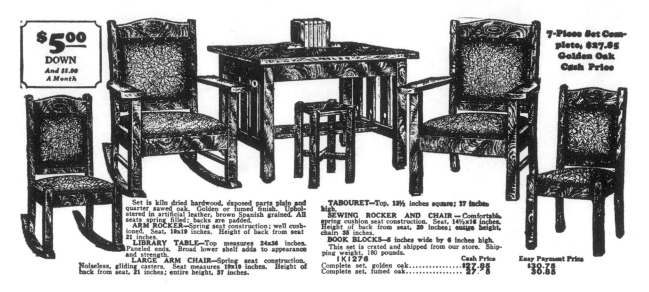

7-Piece Set Complete, $27.85 Golden Oak Cash Price

Set is kiln dried hardwood, exposed parts plain and quarter sawed oak. Golden or fumed finish. Upholstered in artificial leather, brown Spanish grained. All seats spring filled; backs are padded.
ARM ROCKER—Spring seat construction; well cushioned. Seat, 19x19 inches. Height of back from seat 21 inches.
LIBRARY TABLE—Top measures 24x36 inches. Paneled ends. Broad lower shelf adds to appearance and strength.
LARGE ARM CHAIR—Spring seat construction. Noiseless, gliding casters. Seat measures 19x19 inches. Height of back from seat, 21 inches; entire height, 37 inches.

TABOURET—Top, 13½ inches square; 17 inches high.
SEWING ROCKER AND CHAIR—Comfortable, spring cushion seat construction. Seat, 14½x16 inches. Height of back from seat, 20 inches; entire height, chair 35 inches.
BOOK BLOCKS—5 inches wide by 6 inches high. This set is crated and shipped from our store. Shipping weight, 180 pounds.

1K1276	Cash Price
Complete set, golden oak	$27.85
Complete set, fumed oak	27.85

Easy Payment Price $30.75 30.85

149. Nearly fifteen years after Gustav Stickley was forced to declare bankruptcy, the public was still in the market for the popular Mission-style furniture. Sewing rockers and arm rockers in this 1927 Sears, Roebuck illustration were recommended for the living room or library. The austere designs could be compatible with modern interiors.

tial oak pieces might last entirely too long, a "Lifetime" as the name of one Michigan company boastfully suggested. Others predicted its demise on the basis of its radical simplicity:

> The present Mission style is, of course, a fad; not yet, however, in its most virulent and rabid stage, but it already has its champions who make all sorts of claims for it and judging from them it will soon crowd out all other styles. The Mission style is an extreme. We arrived at the Mission style on the principle of the pendulum swing, for fads swing from one extreme to the other as unerringly as does the pendulum. When a start was made away from the elaborately carved, vulgarly ornated styles it was inevitable that the movement would not stop short of something such as the Mission style. The artistic is not to be found at either end of the swing.[7]

The *Craftsman*, the magazine begun by Gustav Stickley in 1901, continued to dispense news, knowledge, and advice until December of 1916, but the Mission movement was already on the wane. In the previous year the Gustav Stickley empire had fallen into bankruptcy as, in every period, furniture fashions were changing. New versions of "quaintness," namely Colonial and pseudo-colonial, gave the public new approaches to decorating, although Mission furniture continued to be made until the 1930s. Some manufacturers of the Mission styles began to market their designs as "Colonial" in order to compete with the increasingly popular antique styles. The association of "Colonial" with Mission furniture was probably derived from the understanding that its roots were in the Spanish colonial missions of California.

150. Grand Rapids, Michigan, was the center of furniture production in the Midwest, and two of Gustav Stickley's younger brothers, George and Albert, moved there in 1891 to establish the Stickley Brothers Company. Much of their production after 1900 consisted of pieces in the Craftsman style of their more famous brother.

The Colonial Manner

For all its popularity, the Mission style was not, of course, for everyone. At least as early as the 1876 Centennial Exhibition, Americans had demonstrated a renewed interest in the artifacts and furniture of their ancestors. The manufacturer of home furnishings in the "Colonial" manner gave the wares respectability, the cachet of venerability despite the lingering odor of new varnish. In 1884, a writer in *Cabinet Making and Upholstery* noted that "The manufacture of antiques has become a modern industry." The reproductions, however, made more than a few concessions to authenticity. In most cases they could claim to be "inspirations" rather than true reproductions.

The common use of rocking chairs in the "Early American" style was suggested in Alice M. Kellogg's *Home Furnishing* (1905), a volume in which their suitability in music, bed, guest, reception, servant's and living rooms was recommended:

The "livable" element would be defeated if the individual requirements of the family were not recognized in the selection of the furniture. Yet a preference for rockers, Morris chairs, low seats or high backs, soft cushions or hard wood need not be gratified at the expense of good style, for a wide range is at hand from colonial designs to the modified mission of the present day... A plain, comfortable rocker is not easy to find, but one may be searched for in a flag seat or an upholstered seat and back, that is not too ornate for its position.

Quaintness and Nostalgia

The benevolent aspect of the modern antiques industry in the twentieth century can be epitomized by the Framingham, Massachusetts, empire of Wallace Nutting.[8] A prominent early collector and author, Nutting manufactured a large number of reasonably close copies of Pilgrim and eighteenth-century furniture between 1917 and 1936. In addition, many thousands of hand-tinted photographs signed "Wallace Nutting" were marketed, illustrating "Colonial Interiors" from the bygone days. Romantically rustic, the interior settings featured period and reproduction furniture and accessories which unquestionably fueled the public's appetite for the Nutting products. Rocking chairs were sometimes used in these photographs to help lend an atmosphere of quaintness and to reinforce the assumption of comfort in an earlier age. Even though the rocking chair had not been a common furniture form in the Colonial period, it had by 1900 become associated with what was perceived as a more tranquil past. James C. Beckel's song "Old Easy-Chair by the Fire" captured that nostalgic mood "Moderato espressivo":

Oh, she was my guardian and guide all the day,
And the angel that watched round my bed.
Her voice in a murmur of prayer died away
For blessings to rest on my head.
Then I thought ne'er an angel that Heaven could know,
Tho' trained in its own peerless choir,
Could sing like my mother, who rocked to and fro
In the old easy-chair by the fire.

How holy the place, as we gathered at night
Round the altar where peace ever dwelt,

151. *Anne in White*, c. 1920, an oil on canvas by George W. Bellows (1882-1925), depicts a child posed in her simple slat-back rocking chair. That style had already been popular for nearly two hundred years when Anne sat for her portrait.

152. The "reproduction" of Colonial furniture occasionally resulted in unlikely combinations of elements from the past. An eighteenth-century counterpart to this model is unknown and highly unlikely. Made and labeled by C. F. Meislahn & Company, Baltimore, about 1880.

To join in an anthem of praise, and unite
In thanks which our hearts truly felt!
In his sacred old seat, with his locks white as snow,
Sat the venerable form of my sire,
While my dear mother sat as she rocked to and fro
In the old easy-chair by the fire.

Many other furniture manufacturers besides Nutting made reproductions with varying degrees of success, but the infatuation with historic furniture styles was not without its critics. By 1930, the Tulsa, Oklahoma *Tribune* was moved to editorialize:

Pretty much of the antique craze is cheap intellectual affectation. There is a lot of bunk about it. Isn't it absurd to stage-set the parlor; we aren't playing King Lear. We make better boxes in the twentieth century than were made in Chaucer's time, just as our pianos today are better than the old harpsichord. It is absurd to assume that when we come to beds, hall boxes and dining boards, we have lost the art of furniture design and craftsmanship. Must we go back to hand-hewn timbers to find beauty in furniture? As a curiosity the old junk has value, and the older it is the greater the historical value. But it all belongs in the museum much more than in the home.[9]

153. The drawing of a young mother and child in a "Colonial" Revival rocking chair by William Glackens (1870-1938) was used to illustrate the Alva Kerr story "Muggins Lorney's Tinkerings" in *The Saturday Evening Post* (December 19, 1903).

154. *Right:* This "Colonial Rocker" was advertised as "suitable alike for lady or gentleman, young or old, and for any room in the home," when the Fred Macey Company, Grand Rapids, Michigan, offered it in its *Christmas Gifts* catalogue about 1902.

155. "A Mother! How Odd!" This satirical comment on "the apes of fashion" appeared in *Puck*, c. 1905. The artist, Gordon Ross, knowingly places his virtuous young mother in a rocker.

Despite such negativism, antiques and their more-or-less faithful copies continued to be popular. Due, perhaps, to their quaint appeal, rocking chairs were among the most frequently advertised pieces of furniture. Windsor-style rockers were offered by many manufacturers, but in most cases they were improved with fancy turnings and steam-pressed, "carved"-oak top rails. The pure lines of the originals were too ordinary and plain to completely suit modern customers who liked to see some sign of technological advancement. After all, if the old was good, could

not its reincarnation be just a little bit better? In some cases, though, the innovations so dominated the piece that the original conception was obscured in a profusion of machine turning and carving.

Rocking chairs were created in the first decades of the twentieth century that could claim a variety of ancestors for the same chair. It was possible to find a fancy spindled Windsor rocker with a rolled seat borrowed from the Boston rocking chair combined with a Queen Anne or Chippendale back splat (figure 156). Authenticity was not a major

156. The rocking chair on the left features a combination of elements, including a Boston-type rolled seat on a frame of vague Mission design, and the right hand example is an "improved" Boston rocker in the style popular at the turn of the century. Both were pictured in the 1900-1901 catalogue of The Wisconsin Chair Company of Port Washington, Wisconsin.

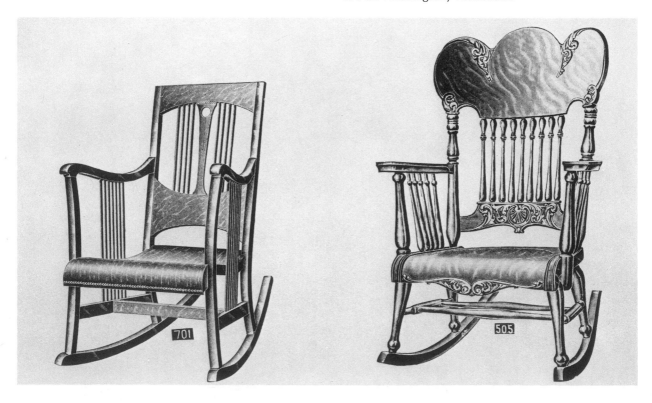

concern of most of the public, and, consequently, the manufacturers felt few constraints on their imaginations. The taste, generally, ran to an elaboration of the original form. Modern technology permitted mass production of furniture which featured simulated carved designs that would have been very expensive in the eighteenth century if created by a master craftsman. Consequently, chairs which were patterned after high-style Queen Anne or Chippendale examples could be offered with or without rockers, although originally they were formal, expensive pieces of furniture never made as rocking chairs.

It is clear that by the twentieth century the rocker had achieved such a high level of acceptance that no historical style was considered inap-

propriate for adaptation. The classic American periods were often used, but a demand for more exotic styles was also exploited. In S. Karpen and Brothers' thirty-third annual furniture catalogue of 1913, numerous rocking chairs were advertised. The "English" model wing-chair rocker with cane seat and back could claim origins in the William and Mary period of the late seventeenth century. "Sheraton" rocking chairs, with upholstered or caned seats and backs, were based on the late eighteenth-century designs of Thomas Sheraton. Customers with even more elaborate decorating schemes could choose from "Louis XVI," "Renaissance," and "Turkish" rocking chairs, which provided "comfort insurance." Literary history was raided, too, and Washington Irving's

157. Two fancy pressed-back rocking chairs, which, except for the backs, share the same design, were illustrated in the 1900-1901 catalogue of The Wisconsin Chair Company. These elaborate chairs would have been suitable for a fashionable middle-class parlor.

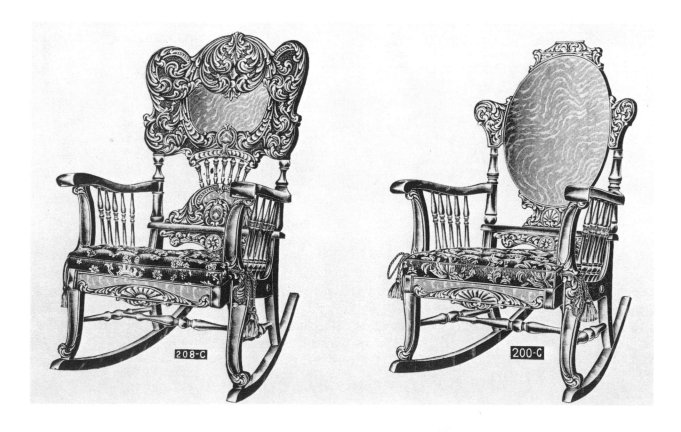

Beautiful Blended Walnut Bedroom Set

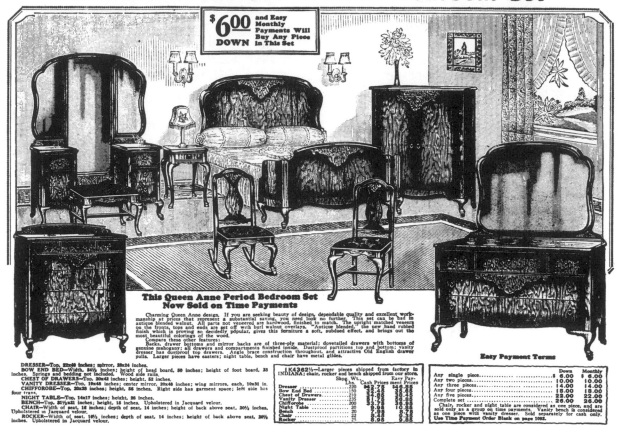

158. In 1927 the Sears, Roebuck and Company mail-order catalogue advertised this "Period Bedroom Set" in a "Charming Queen Anne design" and with "antique blended walnut" finish. The manufacturer of Colonial furniture still provides the consumer with a popularly-priced link to the American past in varying degrees of authenticity.

The Sketch-Book inspired the "Sleepy Hollow" reclining rocker.

The popularity of these pieces in antique styles has persisted throughout the twentieth century. Sears, Roebuck & Company, "The World's Largest Store," illustrated a "Queen Anne Period Bedroom Set" in its 1927 catalogue that included a matching rocking chair upholstered in jacquard velour (figure 158). Windsor rockers could be purchased that were "Patterned after an original old English design," despite the fact that no prototypes existed. A number of "comfortable rockers" that resembled American eighteenth-century easy chairs were sold upholstered in a choice of ar-

158

159. Mrs. D. had snapshot postcards made in 1908 of her fancy parlor in Hyndsville, New York. The implied sense of comfort and well-being is reinforced by the heavily carved center table, oriental carpet, and the rocking chairs in profusion.

tificial leather, jacquard velour, or mohair. An added convenience, unknown to eighteenth-century Americans, was an adjustable footrest which could be folded out of sight when not in use. The diversity of these easy-chair rockers in 1927 was an indication of their increased popularity, a popularity which has continued to expand in the past several decades.

Modernism as a trend in furniture design had not become evident to most American furniture manufacturers, although in Europe young designers were already embracing functionalism as the wave of the future. Americans were content with their "quaint" furniture, whether it was plain, sturdy Mission oak or historic mahogany. It is true that a few individuals such as the architect Frank Lloyd Wright and the graphic designer Will Bradley had suggested new approaches to interior design, but they were ignored by the general public.[10] The unmistakable signal for change came from abroad in 1925 with the great Paris International Exhibition of Decorative Arts.

160. "Winter," from the 1956 *Four Seasons* calendar by Norman Rockwell.

6.

Old Rocking Chair's Got Me

The history of modern furniture has been written and studied from many angles. It has, in common with eighteenth-century design, and in contrast to that of the nineteenth century, a certain focus on the individual who created the designs. Pattern books such as those of Thomas Chippendale, Thomas Sheraton, and George Hepplewhite helped to extend the influence of these designers and today their names are even associated with furniture styles only vaguely resembling their original conceptions. Although there are exceptions, the identity of their counterparts in the nineteenth century has been submerged by scholars in an aura of general historicism.

Modern Design

The work of prominent twentieth-century designers promoted a new machine aesthetic. Men like Josef Hoffmann and Marcel Breuer successfully renewed the emphasis on function in furniture embraced earlier by some nineteenth-century furniture engineers. The practical definition of a chair as, first and foremost, a seat which serves to support the body was their concern, rather than the subjective interpretation of the chair as throne or seat of authority to which elaboration is added to enhance the individual's self-image. The romance of functionalism replaced fantasy as the basis of modern design. As Walter Gropius wrote in a typical Bauhaus pronouncement: "In order to create something that functions properly—a container, a chair, a house—its essence has to be explored, for it should serve its purpose to perfection, i.e. it should fulfill its function practically and should be durable, inexpensive, and 'beautiful.'"[1]

An aesthetic developed that emphasized a new cooperation between art and industry. The machine was no longer used primarily to duplicate, or rather simulate, handiwork. Carving and turning were subordinated and an austerity of line and shape was stressed. Nostalgia, therefore, had no place in the strict, impersonal interior of a modern home, and a victim of this approach to design was the rocking chair. Because stability was a chief attribute of the new functionalism, the mobile rocker represented an antiquated informality that was out of time and place.

Thonet's Success

One happy exception to the exclusion of the rocking chair from modern interior decoration was the continued production of a variety of bentwood styles (figure 162). The foremost firm involved in the bentwood tradition continues to be that founded in 1842 in Vienna, Austria, by Michael Thonet. Although the first bentwood rocking chair was manufactured by Gebrüder Thonet in 1860, the chair and its adaptations have been in almost constant production since that time. Continued success is related to the basic emphasis on simple linear patterns rooted in the technological process of bending wood by steam.[2]

In the 1911 Gebrüder Thonet catalogue, printed in six languages, over fifty-five different rocking chairs were illustrated. All used bent wood to some degree, but perforated veneer backs, carved classical urn motifs, and even platform rocker

161. Edouard Vuillard (1868-1940) painted this French interior, c. 1900, a scene that illustrates the continued popularity of the bentwood rocking chair. Although Americans have had hundreds of rocker styles to choose from, Europeans have been content with classic bentwood rockers, and, apparently, thought them compatible even with "antique" styles.

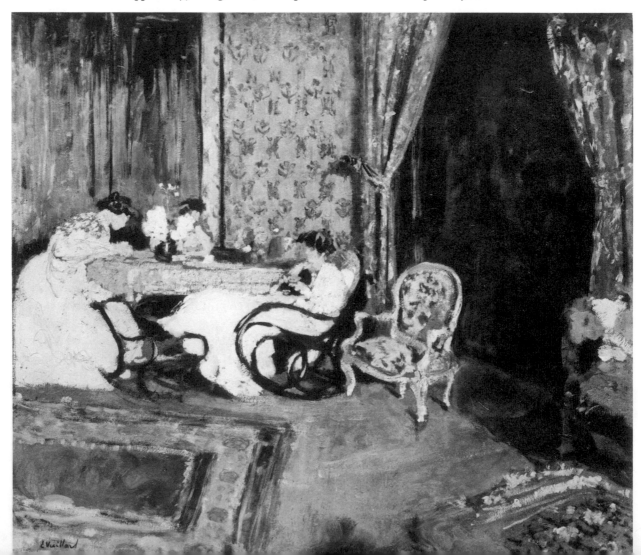

Nr. 7223

mechanisms served to broaden the image of the Thonet rocking chair. After World War II the firm's production facilities located in Poland, Czechoslovakia, and Rumania were appropriated by the Communist regimes, and today Thonet (A Simmons Company) buys its rocking chairs from Poland to distribute in the United States.

By 1930, the rocking chair's fashionableness had been largely eclipsed because of a preoccupation with new styles of seating forms and a corresponding avoidance of quaintness or nostalgia in decoration. As architects assumed a prominence in the aesthetics of home furnishings, furniture became more consciously sculptural. It was natural to desire furniture to complement modern interiors, but few designers attempted to accommodate the rocking chair in their schemes.

162. Thonet Brothers manufactured a wide range of bentwood rocking chairs and, through the company's far-flung sales network, helped to extend the popularity of that form. Thonet's 1913 catalogue was printed in six different languages.

Human Engineering

The late 1930s witnessed changes in the modern furniture movement as a result of an increased importation from Scandinavia. A growing public acceptance of modern design was in part due to the widespread exposure such design received at the Century of Progress exhibition at Chicago in 1933 and the New York World's Fair of 1939. The popularity of Swedish Modern in the late '30s and '40s paved the way for the almost ubiquitous acceptance of Danish Modern in the '50s. Practicality and functionalism were still important factors, but the machined, impersonal architect's furniture was adapted to emphasize natural wood surfaces and a hand-sculptured appearance.

Scandinavian exports included very few rocking chairs, but, recognizing the common tendency for people to tilt back in straight chairs, designers constructed them to withstand the stress. In the 1950s, intensive studies were conducted by Swedish researchers under the auspices of The Swedish Society for Industrial Design to ensure durability and aptness:

They...constructed a machine on which a chair, with a weight of 154 lb. on the seat, is placed. The chair is then tipped back and forth in the same way as it would be in daily use. The number of times it rocks is registered automatically. If the chair can take more than 25,000 rocking movements, it is considered excellent. If it can take only 1,000-10,000 rocking movements it is recommended as a bedroom chair or such. Chairs which fail the test have one or more flaws in construction which can be localized by tests. The producer is informed about the chair's weak points, and in this way has an opportunity to correct them before the chair goes into production.[3]

It would have been much simpler to have designed a real rocking chair than to have tortured straight chairs, but rockers have always had a limited popularity in Scandinavia.

Science gradually affected the appearance of furniture through research and the modern study of ergonomics, or "human engineering" as it is known in America. Many patent furniture engineers of the nineteenth century had carefully considered anatomy in their inventions of various seating forms, but, for the most part, the "transitory" upper-class furniture—as Siegfried Giedion refers to that made in uninventive historical styles—was based primarily on fashion.

A conspicuous exception to transitory furniture through the years has been the rocking chair. Ralph Caplan, critic and writer, has noted that "truly comfortable chairs have generally been a middle-class achievement." And, of course, it is the middle-class desire for comfort that led to the introduction and popularity of the rocking chair in America. The basic factor contributing to the comfort of the rocking chair is that the sitter has the freedom to constantly move his or her body. As a consequence, the force of gravity may be shifted from one part of the anatomy to another, preventing the soreness or fatigue that comes from

sitting motionless for an extended period of time. Support in the lumbar region of the back—the lower five vertebrae—contributes to the success of rocking chairs as comfortable seats.[4]

163. Unusual inlaid mahogany rocking chair, possibly made in Grand Rapids, c. 1920, in a modern rectilinear style.

164

Although most modern furniture designers have chosen not to produce rocking chair forms, a large number of manufacturers have continued to market the traditional or "Colonial" models. Throughout the twentieth century, "Early American" furniture has consistently had a place in manufacturers' catalogues. As in all periods that revive styles from the past, the authenticity may range from precise reproduction to nostalgic concoction never imagined by our ancestors (figure 164). .In the *Old Colony Furniture* catalogue of 1937, for example, the Heywood-

164. The "Bean Pot Rocker" on the left is a fanciful chair which most clearly resembles the popular pressed-back spindled designs popular at the turn of the century. On the right is a modern example of the classic caned Grecian rocking chair, in continuous use since the 1830s.

Wakefield Company of Gardner, Massachusetts, offered rocking chairs in several of the traditional American styles, in contrast to their "Streamline Maple" sold through a separate catalogue which did not feature rocking chairs at all. Most of the popular eighteenth- and nineteenth-century American styles were available, such as the upholstered platform rocker with a helical spring, and the "Lincoln" rocker with upholstered contoured back and spring seat. Both of these chairs were much-simplified adaptations of period examples. Plain, broad wood surfaces were used to update the often elaborate nineteenth-century models of the platform rocker. The Heywood-Wakefield "Lincoln" rocker was a simple Grecian rocker, whereas its namesake had fancy scrolled arms, a carved crest, and buttoned damask upholstery. Heywood-Wakefield also advertised a "Boston Rocker" and brace-back Windsor rocking armchair available in "Priscilla Maple Finish" even though the prototypes were always painted. This concession to naturally finished Windsor chairs reflected the same misinterpretation of our ancestors' taste which resulted in the stripping of original painted finishes from old furniture practiced by many unknowing twentieth-century antiques collectors and dealers.

The influence of antiques collectors on the products of furniture manufacturers is also apparent in the *Antiques of the Future* catalogue (1940) from Bair's Cabinet Shop, Abbottstown, Pennsylvania. The proprietors of Bair's chose to reproduce a local Delaware Valley style slat-back chair, offered with or without arms and each available as rocking chairs. The advertising slogan was meant to appeal to that growing number of Americans who actively sought examples of early furniture decorated in the Colonial taste. It may also have implied craftsmanship and durability in contrast to the so-called "Borax" furniture, which was bulky, poorly constructed and characterized by its

cheap prices. Such "Early American"-styled furnishings could be mixed with authentic antiques, although relatively few customers demanded exact reproductions.

Rocking chairs were a popular item in the *Everything in Furniture* catalogue issued by the Acme Furniture Company of Chicago, Illinois (1901). Fifteen wicker "comfort" rockers in a range of style from plain to very elaborate were produced at the company's southeastern Michigan factory. Even more impressive was their offering of traditional and period rocking chairs, available in nearly every style of chair sold by Acme. The terms used to describe nineteenth-century rockers—"nurse," "ladies sewing," and "Boston"—were retained while their "Colonial" rocking chairs were typically Mission, with leather upholstered seats.

Because traditional furniture has continued to be popular throughout the twentieth century, rocking chairs remain in demand. Among today's manufacturers are several—such as the Tell City Chair Company, Heywood-Wakefield, and Nichols & Stone—which have been producing rockers for at least a century. In the modern furniture market, many different types of companies seek to provide a variety of rocking chair styles. The Tell City (Indiana) Chair Company, a large manufacturer, sells a broad range of "Early American" adaptations, while smaller local businesses, like The Rocker Shop (Marietta, Georgia), continue to make only a couple of rocking chair styles in authentic century-old family designs. In addition, there are a number of individual craftsmen, such as Robert Whitley (Solebury, Pennsylvania), who build limited numbers of rockers by painstaking hand-methods.

The Tell City Chair Company has had a long history of manufacturing traditional furniture. Their rocking chairs have been made in numerous styles since the first simple slat-back "cane

165. The "Farmhouse Rocker" is a design currently made by the Tell City (Indiana) Chair Company. It closely resembles the typical c. 1860 "balloon-back" rocking chair of western Pennsylvania-eastern Ohio which was also produced in the Zoar (Ohio) Communities.

splint" bottom chair was introduced. A planned community of furniture craftsmen, Tell City was founded by a group of Swiss settlers from Cincinnati and was named for their national hero, William Tell. By 1865 a document establishing the Chair Makers Union of Tell City was signed. In the first seventy years of that Union, chairs, including those with rockers, formed the exclusive line, but when "Early American" caught the public's fancy, Tell City began about 1935 to pro-

duce tables, chests, and cupboards. Today, the variety of rocking chairs marketed by this Indiana firm indicates the contemporary interest and demand for "Early American" furnishings. Boston rockers are made in both adult and child's sizes and with several types of decoration. Quite a few upholstered models, including "Rocking Love Seats" and a wide "Rocker-and-a-Half," are manufactured, in addition to a swivel rocking chair and four platform rockers with cushions. A

166. Almost continuously since 1875, the "Brumby Rocker" has been hand-made by local craftsmen at Marietta, Georgia. Five of these oak rocking chairs were recently ordered by First Lady Rosalynn Carter for use in the White House.

"High 'n Easy Rocker" is a modification of the traditional arrow-back Windsor style with shallow-arc runners for limited rocking action and a high seat for ease in standing up. This innovation is intended for part of the rocking chair's traditional constituency, older people and convalescents, but its advantage, "gentle exercise that stretches muscles, stimulates circulation, relaxes tension," has always been applied to rocking chairs in general.[5]

In contrast to the large furniture factories that market numerous styles are many smaller family-owned furniture businesses and individual craftsmen who produce rocking chairs in accurate antique styles or modern adaptations. Ten years after the Civil War, the Brumby family of Marietta, Georgia, designed and produced the first "Brumby Jumbo Rocker" of red oak. Except for a period after World War II, this chair has been made continuously since that time, although the firm, now called The Rocker Shop, is no longer in family hands. Only three rocking chairs and one rocking footstool are sold, and all are plain rockers which make no attempt to "improve" traditional designs (figure 166). The First Lady, Rosalynn Carter, recently ordered five Brumby Rockers for the White House, to be painted white and used on the second floor Truman balcony.[6]

167. William McKinley, twenty-fifth President of the United States, waged his famous front-porch campaign from his wicker rocking chair in Canton, Ohio. Ida McKinley, a frail and epileptic first lady, rocked endlessly at the White House in a small, ornately carved rocking chair which had been hers as a child.

168. The Boston-rocker style has been popular for 150 years. This example, handcrafted by Robert Whitley at his Bucks County, Pennsylvania, workshop, retains the lines of the original. "I see the Whitley Rocker as a contemporary statement, historically rooted in the furniture of the past...I've attempted to achieve a universal truth in its design."

Rocking chairs have often found a place in the White House. President John F. Kennedy, in particular, is associated with the rocking chair because his doctor, Janet Travell, recommended that he sit and relax in a rocker in order to ease back pains from an old war injury. At the National Portrait Gallery in Washington, D.C., the official portrait of President Kennedy depicts him seated in that famous rocker. The publicity generated by Kennedy's use of the rocking chair resulted in a resurgence in its popularity around the country. Presidents Harry Truman, Theodore Roosevelt, and William McKinley are some of the other twentieth-century leaders who found comfort and relaxation in their rocking chairs (figure 167).[7]

Robert Whitley of Solebury, Pennsylvania, is an example of a modern furniture craftsman involved in the production of rocking chairs. He began his woodworking career by helping his father restore damaged antique furniture. Today, he executes reproductions, restores antique examples, and produces an adaptation of early Windsor rocking chairs marketed as the Whitley Rocker (figure 168). While retaining the basic Boston rocker style, it features severely plain turnings, a gently rolled seat, and wide rockers. Another major dif-

169. Reclining rocking chairs have become one of the most admired chairs of the twentieth century. "Early-American" furniture also enjoys great popularity, and this La-Z-Boy rocker-recliner styled as an antique easy chair with wings combines features of both forms.

ference is that the early Boston rocking chairs were always painted, whereas Whitley Rockers of American black walnut, ash, and cherry are given an oil finish to emphasize the wood grain. It is, perhaps, a sign of the times that the humble Boston rocker which cost as little as $3.75 in 1842 has evolved into a piece of designer furniture retailing at more than $1,000.[8]

One of the most successful manufacturers of rocking chairs today, the La-Z-Boy Chair Company of Monroe, Michigan, has concentrated on development of the platform rocker. In 1961 they introduced the "Reclina-Rocker" which com-

bines their popular recliner with the rocking chair, a variation of the nineteenth-century platform rocker, and has become the company's best selling model (figure 169). The company's slogan—"50 Years of Comfort"—indicates the continued emphasis on the upholstered rocking chair's inherent attributes. Recliner-rockers produced by a number of manufacturers in addition to La-Z-Boy have become the most popular of the platform rocking chairs on the market today. Reminiscent of the novel nineteenth-century inventions, one advertised recliner-rocker, the "Catnapper," features a built-in heater and vibrator.

Innovative Technology

There are a number of modern designs for the rocking chair which have had limited success in recent decades, although none has achieved widespread popularity. A variety of materials and processes are utilized, including plastics (especially injection-molded), aluminum, and other metals. One of the earliest of the modern-era rocking chairs was designed by Charles Eames, who, trained as an architect, became the most original American furniture designer of the twentieth century. His earliest rocker was a 1944 molded-plywood lounge chair with cantilevered steel-tube base that had a modest rocking action (figure 171). In 1950 an Eames design for a rocking armchair with a molded polyester body mounted over a rigid wire base and birchwood rockers was first manufactured by Herman Miller, Inc.[9]

Several radically new rocking-chair styles have resulted from the increased use of injection-molding processes in furniture production during the decade of the seventies. A one-piece molded plastic rocker with cantilevered base was designed by Larry Bell of the University of Illinois, and an armchair rocker of molded polyethylene with a removable vinyl cushion is produced by Rotocast Plastic Products of Brownwood, Texas. One indication of the renewed interest in the rocking chair is the number of new ideas submitted in the 1977 annual American Institute of Architects International Chair Design Competition. A significant trend in the development of modern rocking chairs is the incorporation of rockers into the structure of the chair as a whole, emphasizing the sculptural qualities of the chair. Innovative technology has provided the materials and production techniques to enable designers to make radical changes in this traditional form (figure 172).

170. Charlie's seventh "Two-in-One" (four rockers), second bookcase-rocker, and first and only "Bookcase Masterpiece," December 1965. Charlie Garrell, a notable craftsman of the Cumberland Mountain area of southeastern Kentucky, constructed this amazing rocking chair of red oak with white oak rockers, and black walnut pegs and trim. His more typical seven-slat-back rocking armchairs are made without a lathe.

171. Tilt-back lounge chair of molded plywood and metal rod construction
by Charles Eames, c. 1944.

172. Free-shape rocking chair of wood with red leatherette lining, by the twentieth-century architect-sculptor Frederick Kiesler, 1942.

Symbol of an American Past

For the present, the rocking chair is still inextricably connected in the public mind to the past. Nostalgia is still a strong force in the modern world because a known past is perceived as freer and less complicated than the unknown future. The rocking chair is a symbol of those "olden days," and, as such, has become subject to manipulation by advertisers and the media. Television commercials which seek to conjure old-fashioned virtue and wisdom employ rocking chairs as props valued for their authenticity. Older persons are usually sitting in their rockers as they dispense the truths or endorsements of commercial messages, and historical dramas of the American experience often provide characters with rocking chairs. What young mother selling the latest diaper design or baby food can be given any credence unless she rests comfortably in her rocker?

The rocking chair is a potent symbol in commercial advertising because its age-old functions still prevail and because its associations with America's past and present are immutable. Old people continue to claim the rocking chair as a favorite seat. It provides limited but stimulating exercise because it keeps the blood flowing and joints moving and allows for the shift in gravity necessary for comfort during long periods of sitting. Mothers and babies still love the rocking chair because its steady, repetitive movement soothes, calms, and tranquilizes the frailest nerves.

The general familiarity we have with the rocking chair has been responsible for its adoption in common metaphors. An oft-used expression, "He's off his rocker," depends upon a widespread perception of the rocking chair's calming and, curiously, stabilizing effect on the sitter. Even the

173. If your rocker's been consigned to the attic, why not restore it to its rightful place of honor—the parlor, the bedroom, the porch, or wherever you seek the quiet pleasures of relaxation?

imaginative slang language of truck drivers and others who broadcast over citizen's-band radios has included the rocking chair as metaphor. On the highway, the ordinary preoccupation of speeding and watching out for police radar traps has led truckers to form "convoys," long streams of one-minded drivers in which the first and last of the group keep watch for "Smokey the Bear," while the protected and reassured truckers in-between can relax "sittin' in the rocking chair."

The rocking chair, in addition to being a symbol for the wisdom that comes with age and the peaceful stability of family life, is, more importantly, a symbol of America itself. For Americans it represents a bond with their own past, in a historical as well as personal sense. Although Gertrude Stein, for example, chose to live in France for intellectual and aesthetic reasons, she could not detach herself emotionally from America. The novelist Samuel M. Steward, who as a young man in the late 1930s spent two summer holidays with the famous writer and Alice B. Toklas, remembers the deep attachment she had for her wicker rocker:

174. *Tea Time*, a photograph by J.V. Footman of Augusta, Maine, c. 1895.

175. *Opposite:* As an artifact, the rocking chair touches mechanisms deep within us—patterns of memory, taste, and satisfaction. Each facet of its use mirrors aspects of our own society, our very selves.

At Gertrude Stein's chateau in the southeast of France, the great calm stillness of the countryside was broken by four sounds: a solitary bird-cry from the trees along the Ain river down the hill, the tinkling of a cowbell now and then, the great uproar marking arrivals and departures—when Basket the poodle and Pepe the chihuahua added a deep-toned bark and a furious high-pitched yapping to the shouts of Gertrude and Alice. But the fourth sound was the all-pervasive one, the one that went on the greater part of the time and has fastened itself in memory.

It was the gentle noise, the squeaking, the happy song of the wicker rocking chair in which Gertrude always sat after dinner, during the long evenings of conversation with the guests at Bilignin. By the tempo of the sound—sometimes slow as old Time, and sometimes under the pressure of Gertrude's excitement rapid and allegro, punctuating her sentences like the commas she disdained—you could judge just how well or how poorly an evening's talk was going. The rocking chair itself was wicker, with a crosspiece joining the front ends of the rockers to form a foot-

rest; its back was straight and not high enough to give support to the head and neck. It was Gertrude's chair, and Alice never sat in it, nor did any guest. It was the chair in which she rocked while she gave forth her opinions and remarks on literature, life, and the world—while the smoke from Alice's cigarettes and those of the guests drifted out into the blue night-shadows, and our infusions of verveine cooled in the paper-thin porcelain cups. And it was the chair she sat in, squeaking steadily, while one afternoon she read aloud to me in her golden contralto her recently finished child's book, The World is Round. *The sound of the chair was the familiar comforting sound of my childhood, a wholly American sound; and whether she had the chair shipped from America or whether she found it in France, I never knew nor thought to ask. But at this far remove in time the sound of the chair seems like an invisible filament that still connected Gertrude with her homeland and with her own childhood. No wonder that Cecil Beaton photographed her beside it, or that Francis Rose sketched her sitting in it; it was an American symbol, one that Gertrude cherished and loved as deeply as she did the symbolism of the American flag....*[10]

The rocking chair is a *visual* link to the past because its continuous use over 250 years makes it a *physical link* to the American past. No other furniture form is more clearly American in its invention, improvement, and promotion. We cherish it for the pleasure it gives, but also because it is peculiarly ours. In its plainest and most exuberant forms the rocking chair survives and continues to satisfy those who love comfort.

Notes

CHAPTER I

1. Walter Dyer and Esther Fraser. *The Rocking-Chair—An American Institution* (New York: The Century Company, 1928), p.11.

2. Margaret B. Schiffer, *Chester County, Pennsylvania Inventories 1684-1850* (Exton, Pa.: Schiffer Publishing Ltd., 1974), p. 106.
Hampshire County (Mass.) Probate Records, vol. VIII, p. 172 (Courtesy of Kathleen Eagen Johnson).

3. Dr. John Jones, a sixteenth-century English physician, is quoted in M.J. Tucker, "The Child as Beginning and End: Fifteenth and Sixteenth Century English Childhood" in L. deMause, ed., *The History of Childhood* (New York: The Psychohistory Press, 1974), p. 242.

4. Francis Mauriceau and Jacques Guillemeau, seventeenth-century French physicians, are quoted in Joseph E. Illick, "Child-Rearing in Seventeenth-Century England and America," in L. deMause, *History*, p. 307.

5. W. Preyer and William Buchan quoted in Lloyd deMause, "The Evolution of Childhood," in L. deMause, ed., *History*, pp. 31-32.
Mrs. Henry Ward Beecher, *All Around the House; or, How to Make Homes Happy* (New York: D. Appleton & Co., 1879), p. 224.

6. Standard cabinet and chairmakers' prices for 1786, quoted in W. M. Horner, Jr., "A Survey of American 'Wing Chairs,'" *International Studio* 99 (July 1931): 72.

7. Thomas Sheraton, *The Cabinet Dictionary* (London: W. Smith, 1803), p. 20.

8. Wallace Nutting, *A Windsor Handbook* (Old America Company, 1917).

9. For more information on William Beesley and other chairmakers in southern New Jersey, see Deborah D. Waters, "Wares and Chairs: A Reappraisal of the Documents," *Winterthur Portfolio 13* (Chicago: The University of Chicago Press, 1979), pp. 161-173.

CHAPTER II

1. Jane Toller, *Country Furniture* (Newton Abbot: David & Charles, 1973), p. 55. John Gloag, *The Englishman's Chair* (London: Allen & Unwin, 1964), p. 199; and "The Rocking Chair in Victorian England," *Antiques* 99 (Feb. 1971), p. 241.

2. Herman Humphrey, *Great Britain, France and Belgium, A short tour in 1835* (Amherst, 1838) I: pp. 179-180.

3. Frances Anne Butler, *Journal* (London: John Murray, 1835), II: p. 97 (Courtesy of Arlene Palmer).
Harriet Martineau, *Retrospect of Western Travel* (London, 1838), quoted in Z. R. Lea, *The Ornamented Chair* (Rutland, Vt.: Charles E. Tuttle Co., 1960), p. 114.

4. James Frewin, "Notice of Two Rocking Chairs," *Architectural Magazine* V (1838): 664-665.

5. Charles F. Hummel, *With Hammer in Hand: The Dominy Craftsmen of East Hampton, New York* (Charlottesville: The University of Virginia Press, 1968), p. 246.

6. Margaret B. Schiffer, *Furniture and Its Makers of Chester County, Pennsylvania* (Philadelphia: University of Penn-

sylvania Press, 1966), p. 79.

7. Ibid., pp. 132-134.

8. Dean A. Fales, Jr., *American Painted Furniture 1660-1880* (New York: E. P. Dutton & Co., Inc., 1972), see figure 268, p. 167.

9. Sarah Anna Emery, *My Generation*, p. 116, quoted in Fales, *American Painted Furniture*, p. 246.

10. Wright advertisements of October 20, 1830 and November 25, 1831 in *Daily National Intelligencer* (Washington, D.C.), courtesy of Ann Golovin.
Frewin, *op.cit.*

11. Schiffer, *Furniture*, pp. 48 and 134; Gilbert's advertisement quoted in *Made in Utica*, catalogue of an exhibition sponsored by the Munson-Williams-Proctor Institute and the Oneida Historical Society, April 11-September 5, 1976, p. 11.

12. Wright advertisements of January 22, 1829 and August 20, 1830 in *Daily National Intelligencer* (Washington, D.C.), courtesy of Ann Golovin.

CHAPTER III

1. Kenneth Ames, "The Rocking Chair in Nineteenth-Century America," *Antiques* 103 (Feb. 1973): 323.

2. See Ames, p. 325, for illustrations of rocking chairs offered by Phoenix Furniture Company.

3. Hans H. Buchwald, *Form From Process—The Thonet Story* (Cambridge, Mass.: Harvard University Press, 1967).

4. John Gloag, *Antiques, op.cit.*, p. 241.

5. Identical patents for a bent metal rocking chair design were awarded to Herman Berg, Springfield, Mass. (#63,000, March 19, 1867) and Richard Hoffman, New York (#68,627, September 10, 1867). This is a highly irregular practice for the Patent Office; the reasons for its occurrence, however, are unknown.

6. Siegfried Giedion, *Mechanization Takes Command* (New York: Oxford University Press, 1948), p. 390.

7. Daniel Harrington, Philadelphia, Pa., patent granted April 23, 1831. See Giedion, p. 402, for illustration.

8. Charles Grawitz, Buffalo, New York, Patent #108,255, issued October 11, 1870.
Abel Russell, Brooklyn, New York, Patent #136,099, issued February 18, 1873. See Ames, p. 326, for illustration of Russell's rocking chair.

9. Martin Eberhard, Philadelphia, Pa., Patent #16,006, issued November 4, 1856.

10. T. W. Currier, Lawrence, Mass., Patent #19,352, issued February 16, 1858.
A. S. Smith, Lawrence, Mass., Patent #20,376, issued May 25, 1858, and reissued June 27, 1865.

11. Samuel H. Bean, Philadelphia, Pa., Patent #1,531, issued March 31, 1840.

I.P. Carrier, South Glastonbury, Conn., Patent #20,863, issued July 13, 1858.

12. J. Beiersdorf, *25th Annual Illustrated Catalogue* (Chicago, January 1882). Smithsonian Institution Collection of Business Americana.

13. Theodore J. Palmer, New York, Patent #102,701, issued May 3, 1870. Prices for frame and upholstery from *Kimball's Book of Designs* (1876).

14. Butler Brothers, *Specialties in Furniture* (Chicago, Fall and Winter 1891-92). Smithsonian Institution Collection of Business Americana.

15. David Selleg, Newburgh, New York, Patent #201,129, issued March 12, 1878.

16. Clifford C. Nichols, Cincinnati, Ohio, Patent #201,440, issued March 19, 1878.
Nicholas, Claudius, and Adam Collignon, Closter, New Jersey, Patent #176,929, issued May 2, 1876.

17. Charles Horst, New Orleans, La., Patent #5,231, issued August 7, 1847.
Martin Steifenhofer, New York, Patent #89,897, issued May 11, 1869.

18. Mary Ann Woodward, Palmyra, New York, Patent #6,375, issued April 24, 1849.
David Kahnweiler, Wilmington, N.C., Patent #18,696, issued November 24, 1857.

19. Charles Singer, South Bend, Ind., Patent #92,379, issued July 6, 1869.

20. Clayton Denn, Frankford, Pa., Patent #106,790, issued August 30, 1870.

21. Peter Ten Eyck, New York, Patent #9,620, issued March 15, 1853.
P.G. Ingersoll, Greenpoint, New York, Patent #127,888, issued June 11, 1872.

22. P.C. Lewis, *Rip Van Winkle Reclining Rocker* (Catskill, New York, n.d.). Smithsonian Institution Collection of Business Americana.

23. Samuel S. Singer, Sterling, Mass., Patent #7,418, issued June 4, 1850. See also Olive Crittenden Robinson, "A Convertible Boston Rocker," *American Collector* 11 (September 1942): 12-13.

24. Craig Gilborn, "Rustic Furniture in the Adirondacks, 1875-1925," *Antiques* 109 (June 1976): 1218.

25. The Old Hickory Chair Company, *Old Hickory* (Martinsville, Ind., 1901). Smithsonian Institution Collection of Business Americana.

CHAPTER IV

1. For a full survey of the history of Cherry Hill and its inhabitants, see Roderic H. Blackburn, *Cherry Hill: The History and Collections of a Van Rensselaer Family* (Historic Cherry Hill, 1976).

CHAPTER V

1. N. I. Bienenstock, *A History of American Furniture* (New York: Furniture World-Furniture South, 1970), p. 97.
2. John Ruskin, *The Seven Lamps of Architecture* (1849); Charles Lock Eastlake, *Hints on Household Taste* (1868); Robert Judson Clark, *The Arts and Crafts Movement in America 1876-1916* (Princeton: Princeton University Press, 1972).
3. Gustav Stickley, "The Craftsman Designs: Why We Do Not Put Out New Things Merely For the Sake of Variety," *Craftsman* 17 (1910): 698.
4. Bienenstock, p. 98.
5. Ibid., p. 104.
6. Gustav Stickley, "A New Year's Greeting to the Friends of the Craftsman," *Craftsman* 17 (1910): 463.
7. Bienenstock, pp. 100-101.
8. William L. Delaney, "Wallace Nutting: Collector and Entrepreneur," *Wintherthur Portfolio 13* (Chicago: University of Chicago Press, 1979), pp. 47-60.
9. Bienenstock, p. 117.

CHAPTER VI

1. Peter Bradford, *Chair* (New York: Thomas Y. Crowell, 1978), p. 11.
2. Buchwald, *op.cit.*; and Thonet Industries, *The Thonet Story* (brochure, York, Pa., n.d.)
3. Ulf Hård af Segerstad, *Modern Scandinavian Furniture* (Totowa, N.J.: The Bedminster Press, 1963), p. 57.
4. Bradford, p. 16.
5. Tell City Chair Company, *We Aim To Make Good Furniture* (historical booklet, n.d.).
6. The Rocker Shop, *Georgia's Brumby Heritage* (brochure, 1976); and "Rockers Returning to White House," *Savannah Morning News*, April 2, 1977.
7. Amy LaFollette Jensen, *The White House and Its Thirty-four Families* (New York: McGraw-Hill Book Co., 1965).
8. Robert Whitley, *The Whitley Rocker* (booklet, Solebury, Pa., 1978).
9. Arthur Drexler, *Charles Eames Furniture from the Design Collection, The Museum of Modern Art, New York* (New York: The Museum of Modern Art, 1973), p. 34.
10. Samuel M. Steward, "The Little Sounds of Bilignin," written expressly for publication in *The Rocking Chair Book*. Mr. Steward's friendship with the two famous women is recounted in *Dear Sammy: Letters From Gertrude Stein and Alice B. Toklas* (Boston: Houghton Mifflin Company, 1977).

Bibliography

Ames, Kenneth, "The Rocking Chair in Nine-teenth-Century America," *Antiques* 103 (Feb. 1973): 322-327.

Baroody, Elizabeth, "Easy Comfort: Rocking Chairs," *The Antiques Journal* 34 (Jan. 1979): 38-40

Bienenstock, N. I., *A History of American Furniture*. New York: Furniture World-Furniture South, 1970.

Bishop, Robert. *Centuries and Styles of the American Chair 1640-1970*. New York: E. P. Dutton & Co., Inc., 1972.

Boots, Edmund R. *Rocking Chairs by Ben Franklin*. Privately Printed, 1940.

Bradford, Peter. *Chair*. New York: Thomas Y. Crowell, 1978.

Buchwald, Hans H. *Form From Process—The Thonet Chair*. Cambridge, Mass.: Harvard University Press, 1967.

Clark, Robert Judson. *The Arts and Crafts Movement in America 1876-1916*. Princeton, New Jersey: Princeton University Press, 1972.

Cummings, John, "Rocking Chairs Before 1840," *Spinning Wheel* 22 (Sept. 1966): 14-15ff.

deMause, Lloyd, ed. *The History of Childhood*. New York: The Psychohistory Press, 1974.

Dyer, Walter A. and Fraser, Esther Stevens. *The Rocking-Chair—An American Institution*. New York: The Century Company, 1928.

Fales, Dean A., Jr. *American Painted Furniture 1660-1880*. New York: E. P. Dutton & Co., Inc., 1972.

Fitzgibbons, Ruth Miller, "Early Rocking Chairs in America: Stepchildren of the Antique World." *American Art & Antiques* 1 (July-Aug. 1978): 106-113.

Freeman, John Crosby. *The Forgotten Rebel: Gustav Stickley and His Craftsman Mission Furniture*. Watkins Glen, N.Y.: Century House, 1966.

Gaines, Edith, "The Rocking Chair in America," *Antiques* 99 (Feb. 1971): 238-240.

Giedion, Siegfried. *Mechanization Takes Command: A Contribution to Anonymous History*. New York: Oxford University Press, 1948.

Gloag, John. *The Englishman's Chair: Origins, Design, and Social History of Seat Furniture in England*. London: Allen & Unwin, 1964.

_____. "The Rocking Chair in Victorian England," *Antiques* 99 (Feb. 1971): 241-244.

Hecksher, Morrison. *In Quest of Comfort: The Easy Chair in America*. New York: The Metropolitan Museum of Art, 1971.

Jensen, Amy LaFollette. *The White House and Its Thirty-four Families.* New York: McGraw-Hill Book Company, 1965.

Jones, Michael Owen. *The Hand-Made Object and Its Maker.* Berkeley: The University of California Press, 1975.

Kane, Patricia E. *300 Years of American Seating Furniture.* Boston: New York Graphic Society, 1976.

Makinson, Randell L. *Greene and Greene: The Architecture and Related Designs of Charles Sumner Greene and Henry Mather Greene, 1894-1934.* Los Angeles Municpal Art Gallery, January 27-March 6, 1977.

Meader, Robert F. W. *Illustrated Guide to Shaker Furniture.* New York: Dover Publications, Inc., 1972.

Peterson, Harold L. *Americans at Home.* New York: Charles Scribner's Sons, 1971.

Saxe, Thomas E., Jr. *Sittin', Starin' 'n' Rockin'.* New York: Hawthorn Books, Inc., 1966.

Acknowledgments

The Rocking Chair Book was conceived during the winter of 1977-78 through a graduate seminar in Victorian furniture taught by Kenneth Ames as part of the Winterthur Program in Early American Culture of the Henry Francis du Pont Winterthur Museum. Since then, Dr. Ames has been involved with the project through kind counsel, by critically reading the manuscript, and, finally, by writing a thoughtful introduction. We are grateful for his continued friendship.

To our editors, Martin Greif and Lawrence Grow, we are most thankful for their willingness to take on the project and for their ceaseless efforts to carry it to completion.

Finally, we also wish to thank the following friends, scholars, and institutions for their encouragement, assistance, and cooperation: Arlene Palmer, Samuel M. Steward, Ann Golovin, Kathleen Eagen Johnson, Gary and Nancy Stass, Jerry and Jan Paul, Michael Owen Jones, Nina Fletcher Little, Patricia Miller, Todd Volpe, Walt and Joan Burstyn, Robert Peck, Ellen Rosenthal, Sandra Mackenzie, Felice Jo Lundman, Cheryl Robertson, Alice Cooney Frelinghuysen, Robert St. George, Edward S. Cooke III, Spiros Zakas, and Mrs. M. Gentile; Kathryn McKenney, Deborah Waters, Beatrice Taylor, Neville Thompson, Karol Schmiegel, and Alberta Brandt of the Henry Francis du Pont Winterthur Museum; Rodris Roth and Susan Myers of the Smithsonian Institution; Christina Nelson of the Henry Ford Museum; June Burns Bové of the Friends of the Hermitage, Inc.; Philip Curtis, Audrey Koenig, and Carolyn Hughes of the Newark Museum; Randell Makinson of the Gamble House; Gervis S. Brady of the Stark County Historical Society; Margaret S. Cheney of the Mark Twain Memorial; Ann du Mont, Pocumtuck Valley Memorial Museum; Bryant F. Tolles, Jr., The Essex Institute; Sandra Tatman, The Athenaeum of Philadelphia; J. Kenneth Jones, The Charleston Museum; Ann Baker and Ann Fullmer, Division of Historical and Cultural Affairs, Delaware Department of State; Ann G. Perry, The Fraunces Tavern; W.D. Frankforter, Grand Rapids Public Museum; Phyllis McCullough, Thonet Industries; Paige Adams Savery, The Stowe-Day Foundation; Joseph B. Zywicki, Chicago Historical Society; Phillip Johnston and Laura Fecych, The Wadsworth Atheneum; Cynthia Young, The Detroit Historical Museum; Dukes County (Mass.) Historical Society; National Gallery of Art, Index of American Design; Abby Aldrich Rockefeller Folk Art Center; Maryland Historical Society; The Metropolitan Museum; The Shelburne Museum; The Monmouth County (N.J.) Historical Association; Historic Deerfield, Inc.; Worcester Art Museum; Colonial Williamsburg; New Jersey Historical Society; The Whaling Museum, Old Dartmouth Historical Society; State Historical Society of Wisconsin; The Cooper Union; Morris Museum of Arts and Sciences; Historic Cherry Hill; Museum of Art, Carnegie Institute; The Museum of Modern Art; The Campbell House Museum; Archives of Brown & Bigelow; Sotheby Parke Bernet, Inc.; Hammer Galleries; La-Z-Boy Chair Company; George B. Bent Co., Inc.; The Rocker Shop; The Whitley Studio; Tell City Chair Company; and Rotocast Plastic Products.

Credits

1. Private Collection. 2. Mark Twain Memorial, Hartford, Connecticut. 3. National Gallery of Art, Washington, D.C., gift of Edgar William and Bernice Chrysler Garbisch. 4. Historic Deerfield, Inc., Deerfield, Massachusetts. 5. The Henry Francis du Pont Winterthur Museum. 6. Courtesy, Monmouth County Historical Association, Freehold, New Jersey. 7. The Shelburne Museum, Shelburne, Vermont. 8. Collections of Greenfield Village and the Henry Ford Museum, Dearborn, Michigan. 9. Worcester Art Museum, Worcester, Massachusetts. 10. The Henry Francis du Pont Winterthur Museum, gift of H. Rodney Sharp. 11. Index of American Design, National Gallery of Art, Washington, D.C. 12. Courtesy, Monmouth County Historical Association, Freehold, New Jersey. 13. Private Collection. 14. Courtesy, Monmouth County Historical Association, Freehold, New Jersey. 15. Private Collection. 16. Colonial Williamsburg. 17. The Henry Francis du Pont Winterthur Museum. 18. Courtesy, The Old Court House, New Castle, Delaware. 19. Courtesy, Monmouth County Historical Association, Freehold, New Jersey. 20. Private Collection. 21. The Henry Francis du Pont Winterthur Museum. 22. Copyright, Sotheby Parke Bernet, Inc., New York. 23. The Henry Francis du Pont Winterthur Museum, gift of Charles K. Davis. 24. Smithsonian Institution, Washington, D.C. 25. Collection of Gary and Nancy Stass. 26. Collections of Greenfield Village and the Henry Ford Museum, Dearborn, Michigan. 27. John Paul Remensnyder Collection of American Stoneware, Smithsonian Institution. 28. The National Gallery of Art, Washington, D.C., gift of Edgar William and Bernice Chrysler Garbisch. 29. The Henry Francis du Pont Winterthur Museum. 30. Abby Aldrich Rockefeller Folk Art Center, Williamsburg, Virginia. 31. The Henry Francis du Pont Winterthur Museum. 32. The Charleston Museum, Charleston, South Carolina. 33. Copyright, Sotheby Parke Bernet, Inc., New York. 34. Maryland Historical Society. 35. National Gallery of Art, Washington, D.C., gift of Edgar William and Bernice Chrysler Garbisch. 36. The Metropolitan Museum of Art. 37. The Henry Francis du Pont Winterthur Museum. 38. The Shelburne Museum, Shelburne, Vermont. 39. The Henry Francis du Pont Winterthur Museum, gift of H. Rodney Sharp. 40. Collections of Greenfield Village and the Henry Ford Museum, Dearborn, Michigan. 41. Pocumtuck Valley Memorial Association, Deerfield, Massachusetts. 42. Private Collection. 43. Abby Aldrich Rockefeller Folk Art Center, Williamsburg, Virginia. 44. Courtesy, Monmouth County Historical Association, Freehold, New Jersey. 45. Index of American Design, National Gallery of Art, Washington, D.C. 46. Ibid. 47. The Essex Institute, Salem, Massachusetts. 48. Collections of Greenfield Village and the Henry Ford Museum, Dearborn, Michigan. 49. Private Collection. 50. Smithsonian Institution Collection of Business Americana. 51. Dukes County Historical Society. 52. The Shelburne Museum, Shelburne, Vermont. 53. Smithsonian Institution Collection of Business Americana. 54. Winterthur Museum Libraries. 55. Ibid. 56. Smithsonian Institution, Washington, D.C. 57. Smithsonian Institution Collection of Business Americana. 58. Ibid. 59. Ibid. 60. Winterthur Museum Libraries. 61. Pictorial Materials Collection, Grand Rapids Public Museum, Grand Rapids, Michigan. 62. Collections of Greenfield Village and the Henry Ford Museum, Dearborn, Michigan. 63. Smithsonian Institution Collection of Business Americana. 64. Courtesy, Thonet Industries, York, Pennsylvania. 65. Morris Museum of Arts and Sciences, gift of Mr. and Mrs. Bruce Bogert. 66. The Cooper Union, New York City. 67. Smithsonian Institution Collection of Business Americana. 68. Courtesy, The Campbell House Museum, St. Louis, Missouri. 69. Smithsonian Institution, Washington, D.C. 70. Winterthur Museum Libraries. 71. Ibid. 72. Commerce Department, Patent and Trademark Office. 73. Sons of the Revolution, Fraunces Tavern Museum, New York City. 74. The Whaling Museum, New Bedford, Massachusetts. 75. Winterthur Museum Libraries. 76. Smithsonian Institution Collection of Business Americana. 77. Winterthur Museum Libraries. 78. Smithsonian Institution Collection of Business Americana. 79. Courtesy, The Newark Museum, Newark, New Jersey. 80. Winterthur Mu-

seum Libraries. 81. Commerce Department, Patent and Trademark Office. 82. Ibid. 83. Authors' Collection. 84. Smithsonian Institution Collection of Business Americana. 85. Ibid. 86. Index of American Design, National Gallery of Art, Washington, D.C. 87. Smithsonian Institution Collection of Business Americana. 88. Ibid. 89. Smithsonian Institution, Washington, D.C. 90. Ibid. 91. Smithsonian Instituton Collection of Business Americana. 92. Copyright, Sotheby Parke Bernet, Inc. 93. Authors' Collection. 94. Smithsonian Institution Collection of Business Americana. 95. Ibid. 96. Collections of Greenfield Village and the Henry Ford Museum, Dearborn, Michigan. 97. Ibid. 98. Courtesy, Friends of the Hermitage, Inc., Ho-Ho-Kus, New Jersey. 99. Smithsonian Institution, Washington, D.C. 100. Pictorial Materials Collection, Grand Rapids Public Museum, Grand Rapids, Michigan. 101. Courtesy, M. Gentile. 102. Private Collection. 103. State Historical Society of Wisconsin. 104. Smithsonian Institution Collection of Business Americana. 105. Courtesy, Monmouth County Historical Association, Freehold, New Jersey. 106. Smithsonian Institution, Washington, D.C. 107. Authors' Collection. 108. Authors' Collection. 109. Ibid. 110. The Henry Francis du Pont Winterthur Museum, gift of the Halcyon Foundation, American Museum in Britain. 111. Authors' Collection. 112. Ibid. 113. The Henry Francis du Pont Winterthur Museum, gift of the Honorable Charles Winn. 114. Smithsonian Institution Collection of Business Americana. 115. Stowe-Day Foundation, Hartford, Connecticut. 116. Courtesy, Monmouth County Historical Association, Freehold, New Jersey. 117. Smithsonian Institution Collection of Business Americana. 118. Courtesy, Monmouth County Historical Association. 119. Courtesy, The Newark Museum, New Jersey. 120. Winterthur Museum Libraries. 121. Commerce Department, Patent and Trademark Office. 122. The Metropolitan Museum of Art, gift of Frederick H. Hatch, 1926. 123. Van Schaick Collection, State Historical Society of Wisconsin. 124. Winterthur Museum Libraries. 125. Ibid. 126. Ibid. 127. Private Collection. 128. Ibid. 129. Smithsonian Institution Collection of Business Americana. 130. Winterthur Museum Libraries. 131. Copyright, Sotheby Parke Bernet, Inc., New York. 132. Courtesy, The Newark Museum, Newark, New Jersey. 133. Private Collection. 134. Smithsonian Institution Collection of Business Americana. 135. Historic Cherry Hill, Albany, New York. 136. Smithsonian Institution Collection of Business Americana. 137. Collections of Greenfield Village and the Henry Ford Museum, Dearborn, Michigan. 138. Private Collection. 139. Chicago Historical Society. 140. Authors' Collection. 141. Authors' Collection. 142. The Gamble House, Pasadena, California; photograph by Marvin Rand. 143. Courtesy, Jordan-Volpe Gallery, New York. 144. Ibid. 145. Ibid. 146. Ibid. 147. Authors' Collection. 148. Ibid. 149. Private Collection. 150. Authors' Collection. 151. Museum of Art, Carnegie Institute. 152. Smithsonian Institution, Washington, D.C. 153. Copyright, Sotheby Parke Bernet, Inc., New York. 154. Smithsonian Institution Collection of Business Americana. 155. Authors' Collection. 156. Winterthur Museum Libraries. 157. Ibid. 158. Private Collection. 159. Authors' Collection. 160. From the archives of and copyright by Brown & Bigelow, St. Paul Minnesota. 161. Museum of Art, Carnegie Institute. 162. Courtesy, Thonet Industries, York, Pennsylvania. 163. Pictorial Materials Collection, Grand Rapids Public Museum, Grand Rapids, Michigan. 164. Courtesy, George B. Bent Company, Inc. 165. Courtesy, Tell City Chair Company. 166. Courtesy, The Rocker Shop. 167. Courtesy, Stark County Historical Society, Canton, Ohio. 168. Courtesy, The Whitley Studio. 169. Courtesy, La-Z-Boy Chair Company. 170. Courtesy, Michael Owen Jones. 171. Collection, The Museum of Modern Art, New York. 172. Ibid. 173. Private Collection. 174. Authors' Collection. 175. Private Collection.

Index